T0063967

SURVIVING IN A DANGEROUS WORLD

TOCHUKWU OKAFOR

SURVIVING IN A DANGEROUS WORLD

iUniverse books may be ordered through booksellers or by contacting:

iUniverse LLC
1663 Liberty Drive
Bloomington, IN 47403
www.iuniverse.com
1-800-Authors (1-800-288-4677)

ISBN: 978-1-4917-4766-7 (sc)
ISBN: 978-1-4917-4767-4 (e)

Library of Congress Control Number: 2014916725

Printed in the United States of America.

iUniverse rev. date: 10/08/2014

CONTENTS

Foreword..vii

Abstract...ix

Introduction...xi

Chapter 1 Doomsday 1

Chapter 2 The Odd Jobs 9

Chapter 3 Irony of Life...15

Chapter 4 The Dangerous Journey.............................23

Chapter 5 Betrayal in Friendships............................35

Chapter 6 Adaptability to Change.............................45

Chapter 7 Doing Prison Time....................................53

Chapter 8 Congestion in Prisons...............................71

Chapter 9 Just Be Vigilant.......................................83

Chapter 10 Living above Misery................................91

Chapter 11 Surviving the Danger..............................97

About This Book 109

Acknowledgments..111

About the Author...113

References 115

FOREWORD

Tough times don't last but tough people do. Problems, difficulties and hardships are a part of everyone's life. How we handle the dangerous terrain of life ultimately determines the outcome of our life.

Surviving in a Dangerous World is a must-read for all. It reflects the potency of pervasive optimism, dogged determination, thick skin, proper perspective and consistent belief in God.

Tochukwu Okafor in this excellent representation of his journey through the dangerous curves of life has personally inspired me and will definitely inspire any reader who goes through this beautiful work.

There is hardly any human that has not seen or will not see tough times in life. Some survive these trying times courageously while others get roped tighter and tighter in the seemingly deadly jaws. This book is a tool highly recommended for all.

Tochukwu has in literary terms confirmed the words of the greatest book on earth Psalm 30:5 which says "Weeping may endure for a night, but joy cometh in the morning." Taking the healthy risk of opening up his journey in life to all, he again reiterates to us that the longest night will always end with a morning.

I will recommend this book to all and sundry as a valuable asset through the inevitable dangerous phases of life.

Above all, to cherish "The Joy of Success" you must learn to survive in this dangerous world.

Dr. Michael Igwe (MD)
President/CEO
Eagles Network International

ABSTRACT

We tend to shy away from our responsibilities simply because we perceive danger. We become uncomfortable with life, people, and work; therefore, we often avoid them. Yes, for sure, it's a dangerous world, where brothers kill one another, strangers kill pedestrians, and even nations rise against their neighbors. But *Surviving in a Dangerous World* encourages you to learn how to swim in troubled waters.

When we let fear of danger sink into our bones, it deprives us of the urge to engage in life activities. Paranoia arises when we are constantly worried about the dangers of this age instead of focusing on how to accomplish our goals. It's true that this book is intended to alert readers to the dangers around us, but it doesn't say to abstain from living a normal life or aspiring to great accomplishments; instead it equips readers with the tools to challenge their fear of danger.

This book exposes how dangerous the world is, but it also presents how to enjoy a quality life regardless. Furthermore, it addresses the need to remain committed to work, participate in social activities, and continue to enjoy family and friends.

Many jobs are deemed particularly dangerous, but take note of one important fact: someone has to do the dangerous jobs to make a dangerous world a little safer. This book includes anecdotes from such situations to mark the fact that survival is possible when one looks beyond the imminent danger.

INTRODUCTION

I am delighted to unveil the fact that we live in a dangerous world. That might seem strange, but when we have awareness of this simple fact—that the world is dangerous—it becomes easy for us to find the best approach to life.

It's also important to know that sometimes what we perceive as dangerous is not actually dangerous. But, because we are human, we tend to run from both real and imaginary danger.

Most would consider prison dangerous, both as a prisoner and as a prison staff member. If a loved one goes to prison, family members are concerned because one can never tell what the outcome will be. If one gets a job at a prison, family members are again worried because of fear of the unknown. They worry not only about physical attacks but also different kinds of diseases prevailing in the prison environment.

Obviously, some people let the fear of danger deter them from having a rewarding career. It continues to bother my mind how almost everyone wants to avoid jobs that are perceived as dangerous.

Some feared jobs like courier industry, corrections, police, fire service, military service, and many more have the best benefits in the world—but you have to earn it. Be it long-term or short-term, financial or medical, you can't ask for anything better after you have courageously and judiciously paid your dues by persevering in an unpleasant work environment.

I have noticed that those who survive in a dangerous work environment are the ones who succeed the most in life. Truly, the hard way is the only way. Those dangers in the world make you stronger as a person.

There are hurdles and challenges we face in life, but our determination to survive is what makes the difference. Life itself is just a journey, which sometimes is not as straight-forward as we wish, but we need to always focus and pay attention to details.

Do not let the challenges of life obstruct your vision as you strive to build a quality life. As Helen Keller said, "Avoiding danger is no safer in the long run than outright exposure."

CHAPTER 1

DOOMSDAY

It was another fall morning in New York City when the world seemed to collapse. The birds ceased singing, the wind stopped blowing, and laughter vanished from people's lives, at least for a time. September 11, 2001, popularly known as 9/11, was the day the enemy struck the World Trade Center (Twin Towers)—highlighting the fact that we live in a dangerous world. The destructive nature of man put America on alert.

Before 9/11, many believed our beloved nation to be untouchable and indestructible. The economy was very strong, and the country was a superpower. The wake-up call reminded us that in the midst of life, there is also death. We were taken unawares as the Iroko trees (Twin Towers) fell to ground zero. The incident sent a warning to everyone: that there is danger wherever you go. Immigrants traveled far and wide to enjoy freedom, peace, and security in the United States, only to face the calamity of 9/11. Tell me where there is no danger; that's where I will go. Guess what? There is danger everywhere.

In the summer of that year, I had come back from Hamburg, Germany, ready for my fall semester at New Jersey City University

(NJCU). The demarcation between Jersey City and New York City is just the Hudson River—a stone's throw. As one who had just flown back to the States without problem, I felt confident about air travel. I wouldn't have expected so much as a plane crash, let alone a terrorist attack.

That day, we were just sitting inside the school lobby as the television flashed, "Breaking news: World Trade Center is hit by an airplane." You would think it was just an accident, right? Momentarily, another plane hit the second tower. That was when the broadcasters concluded that America was under attack. I personally started crying as I watched our financial powerhouse go down. I didn't know where to go and was able only to watch as the Twin Towers melted away like ice.

The sky turned ashy, and the roads grew congested as families ran helter-skelter in search of their loved ones who had gone to work at Wall Street in Manhattan, New York. I walked out of the school building and looked up at the sky; the smoke was too thick to see through. As you might remember, so many people live in New Jersey but work in New York that it became an issue trying to track down family members and friends.

Was it a nightmare? Yes, it was, because the cellular phone lines were down due to the downed signal towers. The roads and bridges were blocked. Anxiety, tension, and fear engulfed the public. President George W. Bush had a sudden interruption to his visit with second graders to tackle the disaster at hand or at least take cover for his own safety.

It was during this incident that the former mayor of New York Rudy Giuliani forged a lasting image. He proved his critics wrong by visibly walking the streets, trying to calm down the chaotic situation. He basically used all available resources in an attempt to get Americans situated in New York and New Jersey because people did not know what to expect next.

The fall of the Twin Towers and two other attacks in the United States on 9/11 claimed almost three thousand lives. The attacks were not planned by a beast; rather, they were masterminded by an intelligent man and executed by able men.

The incident recorded the worst casualties for our firefighters, who voluntarily put their lives on the line, trying to rescue the public. America's financial experts were also drastically reduced when the Twin Towers collapsed.

The following statistics will help us better understand the effect of these deadly attacks, which proved that every inclination of man's heart is evil.

Statistic Verification
Source: 9/11 Commission
Research Date: 9.26.2013
September 11 2001, 19 militants associated with the Islamic extremist group al-Qaeda hijacked four airliners and carried out suicide attacks against U.S. targets. Two planes were flown into the towers of the World Trade Center, a third plane hit the Pentagon, and the fourth plane crashed in a field in Pennsylvania. The attacks resulted in extensive death and destruction, triggering major U.S. initiatives to combat terrorism and defining the presidency of George W. Bush.

Deaths by Area of Attack	Deaths
World Trade Center	2,606
Airlines	246
Pentagon Building	125
Hijackers	19
Total number of people who died in the 9/11 attacks	**2,996**
Casualties in the World Trade Center and Surrounding Area	**Deaths**
Residents of New York	1,762
Persons in North Tower (Tower 1)	1,402
Persons in South Tower (Tower 2)	614
Residents of New Jersey	674
Employees of Marsh Inc.	355
Firefighters	343
Employees of Aon Corporation	175
Port Authority Police Officers	37
Police Officers	23
Paramedics	2
1 firefighter was killed by a man who jumped off the top floors	
Casualties on the Airplanes	**Deaths**
American Airlines Flight 11 (North Tower)	87
United Airlines Flight 175 (South Tower)	60
American Airlines Flight 77 (Pentagon)	59
United Flight 93 (Shanksville, PA)	40
Casualties inside the Pentagon	**Deaths**
Military and civilian deaths	125

As if the memory of 9/11 was not fresh enough anymore, here comes another mystery in this world of confusion. A Malaysian flight traveling from Kuala Lumpur, Malaysia, to Beijing, China, has been reported missing since March 8, 2014. After several weeks of searching, you would think there would be a sign of debris, but the mystery became far from being solved.

I have seen and heard many incredible things but have yet to see an airplane disappear into thin air. The little I know of physics is sufficient for me to know that anything that goes up must surely come down. Now, how can an airplane go up and refuse to land? What magic is behind this?

Under normal circumstances, no one would imagine anything other than an accident, but considering how deviously human minds operate these days, there are strong suspicions that the act was planned and executed. The reason we are privileged to witness or experience certain incidents is so we can remain vigilant at all times.

In the midst of life, brethren, there is danger. Therefore, we should never be ignorant of the devices of Satan. But no matter how dangerous it is to live on earth, we should not be afraid of the unknown. Psalm 23:4 ESV says, "Even though I walk through the valley of the shadow of death, I shall fear no evil."

There is a little bit of risk in everything we do in life. Would you say that because of danger you will not cross the street? When you walk across the street, you take the risk of being hit by a car. Someone who is at home cooking runs the risk of burning down the house. Another who is in the shower could slip and break his head on the bathtub. Our children going to school run the risk of a school massacre. Prison staff run a high risk of being killed by a convicted felon who has nothing to lose. A frequent or even casual flyer faces the risk of a terrorist attack, plane crash, or another form of plane mystery.

Knowing all this should not hinder us from engaging in activities that can make life meaningful and interesting. Rather, they should bring to our attention to the fact that there is someone (a supernatural being) behind our safety and protection. If not for God, who keeps us alive, men would have set the earth on fire, considering how evil the heart of man is.

Psalm 127:1 "Unless the LORD builds the house, the builders labor in vain. Unless the LORD watches over the city, the guards stand watch in vain."

Points to Ponder

1. The world is filled with evil thoughts and evil activities.

2. Even the Bible recognizes the fact that every inclination of man's heart is evil.

3. The tragedy of 9/11 was a wake-up call that sent a message to Americans that in the midst of life, there is also death.

4. We should not feel so comfortable with wealth, economy, and security. Rather, in all things, we should watch and pray.

5. There are always risks in the things we do, and that should not deter us from pursuing our aspirations as well as our daily endeavors.

6. Many lives and hopes were lost, and many finances drastically dwindled after the Twin Tower attack, which highlighted our evil tendency as humans.

7. Most dangers we find ourselves in are created by us, humans. Even though there are natural disasters, bombs, weapons, explosives, terrorist attacks, shooting rampages, and so forth are all artificial destructions.

8. A Malaysian flight traveling from Kuala Lumpur, Malaysia, to Beijing, China, had been reported mysteriously missing, which supports the fact that the world is full of dangerous activities.

9. Even an "untouchable" and "indestructible" nation can go down. Nothing is indispensable.

10. But "even though I walk through the valley of the shadow of death, I shall fear no evil" (Psalm 23:4 ESV). I believe this should be our bedrock as we engage in normal life activities.

CHAPTER 2

THE ODD JOBS

I came to the United States for greener pastures just like every other immigrant. I started my first job at Food Town Supermarket in River Edge, New Jersey. At the supermarket, there were a couple of positions available, and I was given one as a cashier. On my first day, I headed to work with mixed feelings. I liked the fact that I had a job, but I didn't like the fact that I would be a cashier. I just didn't know how it would go, considering that I didn't know the coin denominations. How was I going to count them or give change to customers?

I reported to work and took over the cash register with a long queue of customers standing to pay for their goods. I was ignorant, nervous, and too slow to give change to customers. The computer told me how much change to dispense, but it took me too long to figure out which coin was which. Penny, nickel, dime, quarter didn't make sense to me—poor me.

The bottom line was that I just couldn't cope with the pace and pressure. I was making mistakes—giving away money like crazy, so for my own good, the manager, Martin, moved me to a different department. There I was expected to wash and clean all the dirty areas, including the toilets, meat room, and garbage disposal. I swept the entire supermarket and outside the perimeter. When perishable foods went bad, it was my job to take it out to the Dumpsters.

Twenty-three wasn't really too young to work, but since this was my first time ever working, the wide range of job responsibilities became a little too overwhelming for me. It was just too much work for my skinny self. I even went ahead and got a night job at Amoco gas station in Hasbrouck Heights, New Jersey. After I got off work at Food Town Supermarket, I would go to my gas station night job.

Back to my supermarket job: the meat room (where I spent a good number of hours cleaning) was very cold. I was naturally cold all of the time anyway and then was spending most of my work hours in a freezer room. It was a disastrous experience. But guess what? There was a consolation to it. During my break, I would take all the bad apples, bananas, and grapes (that were supposed to go in the trash) to the restroom, sit comfortably, and just enjoy them. After eating overripe fruit for lunch, I would just crash into a deep sleep (still in the bathroom) until I heard a loud voice in my dream shouting, "Chuchoo! Chuchoo! Chuchoo!" I would wake up; lo and behold, it was not a dream, but one of the employees shouting my name and looking for me. That was how he said my name, Tochukwu. "Here you go again." My long break had been interrupted once again.

Time for a Change

Who enjoys change? Not too many people will tell you they enjoy changing anything, but we should embrace change in order to move forward. Here comes the change in the path of my American Dream. I went through a long, thorough hiring process for acquiring a job with FedEx. I started the job at one of their busy locations in New Jersey. There I found out that my suffering would not be getting any better; instead, it graduated into more physically challenging tasks.

When they told me how much I would be making per hour, it sounded like a lot of money to me. I calculated right away how much it would be after eighty hours. I felt on top of the world. I converted my money into naira (the Nigerian currency) and became instantly rich.

Then came my disappointment discovery that we could only work four hours a day. As an Igbo man (they say it's all about money for this ethnic group), I just wanted to do it full time, eight hours every day plus overtime. It was not until I worked the first and second day that I realized the reason they would not let you work more than four hours per day, never mind eight.

In the middle of work, I noticed I was bleeding from the nose. I was not sick; neither had I been hit by an object nor person. But I was bleeding from too much lifting and dropping while turning my head right to left each second. There was no break in this job, and the fact of the matter was that if you did it for eight hours, you would just die. No two ways about it.

When I finished working and bleeding at FedEx, I would go straight to my Pinkerton security job at Exodus Communications in

Jersey City, New Jersey. (I always held at least two jobs throughout my entire eight-year stay on the East Coast.)

My FedEx job had fantastic benefits. The company not only provided good medical insurance: they also gave you the opportunity to fly anywhere in the world for free. Plus they provided education reimbursement. With all these attractive incentives, one would think that nothing would ever make someone quit such an enticing job, but try it out and see how long you can last. People simply do not last there, notwithstanding the powerful incentives. I tried to hang in there, but it got to a point where it was either die working or resign and go home alive. I chose the latter.

My friend, Dr. Michael Emele, after many years of working for UPS, developed a head-turning syndrome. During his dental school at New York University (NYU), he was also working for UPS. Modern students could not imagine the possibility of a dental student having not only a job but a UPS job. When Dr. Emele had already resigned from this not-so-friendly job, he noticed that his head was always turning left and right, left and right; even while sitting down on a moving bus, he unconsciously turned his head constantly.

I believe the lessons of *Surviving in a Dangerous World* are clear. UPS might be dangerous and strenuous, but today Dr. Emele, in a successful position, has stories to tell about diligence. Indolence has never paid, and indolent people will never have stories to tell their children. Dr. Emele had stories to tell me when I was still new to the country, and I learned from his positive attitude about life.

Those jobs people call "odd jobs" are definitely going to be done by someone. Some people are ashamed of what they do, but that is not necessary as long as you are making money and are striving to do better either through getting more education or through acquiring more work experience to enable you to move forward.

I just can't comprehend how some people can stand still for twenty years. Moving forward or changing direction is my philosophy. I have realized that the higher you go at any workplace, the less strenuous it becomes. You are still going to worry about something, but it will definitely be less of a physical challenge.

Some people will just complain and complain until you are tired of listening. I have really been lucky to have met different types of people. I had the opportunity to meet one who was so pessimistic that he would complain about everybody and everything that happened around him. He would complain about work, school, and all of his friends and relationships.

As Joel Osteen said, "Keep a good attitude and do the right thing even when it's hard. When you do that, you are passing the test. And God promises you your marked moments are on their way."

Points to Ponder

1. Don't feel too big to do the odd jobs, because you have to start somewhere.
2. Don't feel too clean to do the odd jobs, because life is not a bed of roses, especially here in the United States.
3. Don't be afraid to do risky or strenuous jobs, because the rewards are greater, and you are being prepared for greater accomplishments.
4. If a job is going to eat your head, though, run away and save your life.
5. Don't be afraid to embrace change, because change is the most constant thing in life.
6. Indolent people will never have stories to tell. What are you going to tell your children when you have no experiences to share?
7. Don't let fear deter you from getting a rewarding career.
8. Commitment and perseverance keep you on the right path as you challenge the fear of danger.
9. Despite the fantastic benefits of the FedEx job, the strenuous nature of it makes it hard to retain employees.
10. The fear of danger is capable of deterring individuals from having a rewarding career.

Don't let it deter you.

IRONY OF LIFE

The world is just too ironic. Often the person who starts a race slow ends up completing the race before the one who was far ahead. I don't know how long you want to believe that life is just a predictable straight road, but I long ago realized the truth—that life is too ironic to fully understand. It takes sadness to know what happiness is, noise to know what silence is, and absence to value presence.

You might not think, in your wildest imagination, that prison could actually be safer than the outside world. Yes, it can be in some cases! You need to face the reality that today, you can witness shooting rampages in the mall, see a massacre in a movie theater, or see elementary and high school violence as well as domestic violence. There are also incidents of stray bullets killing pedestrians on the streets. It is indeed a dangerous world out there!

I will never forget the day I dropped a big pot of African soup, made by a friend, as I was coming out of my car to enter my apartment building at Elizabeth Avenue in Newark, New Jersey. Why did I drop it? Someone was shooting from a moving vehicle. As soon as I heard the sound of fire, I didn't wait a second to drop what I had, including myself. I believe it is God who protects us, especially on the streets, but you have to do your part for that, and sometimes that includes hitting the ground.

Back to the ironic part of prison work. For the most part, the prison environment is somewhat under control. In most situations, there are enough resources to contain violence or disturbances in prison.

Brian Palmer brought to light that the overall murder rate in Washington, DC, in 2011 was 17.5 per 100,000, which means free people in the nation's capital are more than five times as likely to be murdered than prison inmates. The homicide rate in jails nationwide hovered around 3 inmates per 100,000 between 2000 and 2010, according to data from the Bureau of Justice Statistics. Nationwide, there were 4.7 murders per 100,000 people in 2011, making local jails and state prisons safer than the average American town.

But who would ever imagine that prison was also safer than the street for the inmates (not just innocent people living in dangerous parts of cities)? I have critically evaluated some situations and have determined that some prisoners would have been long dead had they not been imprisoned.

Gang-related drug activities on the street can easily get one killed, but in prison, a gang member or drug dealer can be protected in a cell, where he will have no dealings with his predators or creditors. One of the duties of correctional professionals is to make sure that prisoners complete their prison time alive. Even though some of them want to kill or be killed if given a chance, it rarely happens. Of course, if it *does* happen, someone gets the hit. We strive so hard to prevent it.

One day I entered a big government agency. There were too many people in that building with just one security officer. It had one entrance and one exit despite more than two hundred persons occupying the area. If you entered with a purse, the officer would check it and give it back, but there were no pat-down searches. One could easily come in with a weapon and demolish everyone.

As a security-conscious person, what came to my mind was how dangerous my surroundings were. The place was filled with all kinds of people. I said to myself, "What if anything happens here?" As a matter of fact, if anyone had opened fire, everyone would have perished, including the security officer. That thought reminded me of the fact that what people perceive as safe is often dangerous and vice versa. Prison is perceived by many, if not all, as a very dangerous place to be, but it is safer than many public places. Recreation centers, parks, and mass transit stations are twice as dangerous as prisons.

A police officer once pulled me over and, as soon as he saw my badge, asked me, "Do you work in a prison?"

"Yes, I do," I said.

Don't be shocked to hear what this gentleman said: "I don't know how you guys do it, but I will never work in a prison. It's too dangerous."

A police officer, who is on the street in all weather and sometimes in the middle of nowhere, sees my job—but not his—as a very dangerous one. It's the irony of life. Wonders never cease. What it boils down to is what some people really want to do as well as how people perceive danger. My understanding of danger might be different from yours.

At least in the prisons they have an ICS, which is an incident command system. They also have a TSU, which stands for tactical support unit. They have a CIRT, which means a critical incident response team. They have an A-team, B-team, Dart team, K-9 team, and so many other response teams that are available resources in emergency situations.

Indeed the world is full of contradictions. Most expectations of youth are not met, and many things don't go as planned. A childhood friend of mine, who went to high school in a big city (while mine was in the village), used to take advantage of others because he was a lot savvier and probably smarter than many of us in the village. He was always the instigator of any mischief we carried out. He was pretty sharp and concluded that he would be a pilot when he grew up.

One day, this friend of mine told me that if there was ever civil war in Nigeria, I would die way ahead of him. When I asked him why, he said, "Because you are already too skinny, so by the time I get as skinny as you are, you will have already disappeared into the sand."

Another day, I told him that I would be traveling to the United States (which was quite unbelievable to him) and when I got situated, I would send him some money. He looked at me and said, "What makes you think you will be better than me, to be sending me money?" He claimed that he would not lack anything. "Once I finish my university education, I will move to the Port Harcourt area and start working at Shell Oil Company," he said. At this point, his dream had shifted from being a pilot to working for an oil company.

Lo and behold, I traveled to the United States. One of the first people to call for money was this friend of mine. I sent him the money, which turned out to be a life-changer for him. Things in life don't always go the way we want, and that is why I say that life is filled with unaccomplished expectations and unexpected accomplishments.

I know one girl who said that she would never marry a poor man. She reiterated the need for a rich man by illustrating how she would be running in the rain with an umbrella if she failed to marry someone who had a car. When she thought time was running out, she opened up for any man—even if the man is a pauper.

At Comprehensive Secondary School, Nawfia, Nigeria, there was one particular student who was always dirty and wearing flip-flops instead of sandals. He was abused for constantly looking sloppy. He was never serious with anything. Many thought he would never make it or amount to anything good in life. They gave him the nickname "*legwo*." *Legwo* simply means filthiness combined with sluggishness. He was bullied while in high school. He was emotionally tortured, but that didn't stop him from focusing on his bright future.

Today, *Legwo* has turned out better than the people who had been calling him names. He went to study abroad at the University of Sheffield in the United Kingdom. After his higher education abroad, which included a master's degree, he went back home. He is now happily married and has beautiful children. Even though they live in Nigeria now, he takes his family on vacation to England from time to time. The people that abused him are still struggling to get their bearings in life.

In today's contradictory world, we should not be carried away by our present affluence or our parent's financial buoyancy. Rather, we should always shut our mouths and hope for the best, because life is full of surprises.

The Rise of Udoka

In a remote area of Nigeria, there was a man whose wife gave birth to eight children: seven boys and one girl. Unfortunately, seven out of the eight children died at childbirth, but, as God would have it, the last child survived. Ironically, the day the surviving child, Udoka, was born, her mother died after childbirth. Udoka grew up in the village with her father. She was all her dad had and was doing everything for the man and her uncle. She would perform both male and female jobs around the house, including climbing the palm trees. She had the build of a man, the stature of a warrior, and the spirit of a fighter.

Udoka grew up and remained in the village while her school friends went out to a big city to live a classy and flamboyant lifestyle. One day, all three of her old friends returned home for Christmas and decided to visit Udoka. When they got there, they realized that Udoka was no longer at their level. They could not help but laugh at her. They despised her and humiliated her. They made it clear to her that she was still a village rube, with no class whatsoever.

One day, Udoka went to visit her cousin in Onitsha, and, as she was running away from bandits she encountered on the street, she was discovered by a Nigerian Olympics official. This man came looking for Udoka. He brought the news to her family that they wanted to give her a chance to represent Nigeria in the London Olympics Games in the track and field event. She was taken to Abuja, the new capital of Nigeria, where she outperformed the rest of the girls. She got selected to go to London, and it was such a big deal for her poor father and her struggling cousins.

Lo and behold, a month later, Udoka was seen on television as a Nigerian gold medalist in the 100-meter run in the London Olympics. Her living style changed abruptly. On her arrival to Nigeria, she had a formal reception with the Nigerian government officials, including the president, with tight security surrounding her. She was met with powerful bullet-proof vehicles and a convoy. Even her cousins who came to Abuja to welcome her were all prevented from passing through the gate. They could only wave without knowing which of the black SUVs she was sitting in.

When Udoka finally returned to the village, she built a nice house for her dad and had a huge party in celebration of her victory, while those old friends who thought she had no class came and sat in one corner as they pondered the irony of life.

I will say it again: life is too ironic to boast or brag about anything. Blow not your own trumpet, and let destiny and hard work take you to a desirable destination.

Points to Ponder

1. Life in prison could be safer than life on the street.

2. I am not trying to promote prison as the safest place in the world; rather, I am trying to say that sometimes what you see as danger might not even be the real danger. So when you think that all other public organizations and government agencies are safer than the prison environment, it is not always the case.

3. Life is not a predictable straight road.

4. Develop a mental readiness and physical alertness so as to face the dangers of the world whenever they show up.

5. The people you despise might not be the ones to fail in the future.

6. The contradictions of life are what I refer to as "the irony of life," simply because life doesn't really go as we plan it. Most of us had ambitions regarding what we would be when we grew up, but many of us did not live up to those expectations.

7. Blow not your trumpet, and let destiny and hard work take you to a desirable destination.

8. Life is filled with unaccomplished expectations and unexpected accomplishments. Therefore boast not.

9. Over all, life is full of surprises.

CHAPTER 4

THE DANGEROUS JOURNEY

I will always call it a dangerous journey because I could have died. A journey is dangerous when you don't know where you are going or what to expect on your way. I left Nigeria as a single young man who just wanted to explore the world and get the best out of it. I had no prior arrangements for who would pick me up from the airport, no idea of what the weather would be like, and no clue of where to stay.

Even though the person who promised to sign an affidavit of support for me disappointed me, I was still too positive to quit—probably to my detriment at times. Nothing could have stopped me from coming to America, except God. When the person we knew changed his mind about signing the affidavit, God provided a stranger, who told me, "I will sign it, but it's strictly on business levels. I have a family and we live together in Los Angeles, California. Therefore, I don't want you to live with me. It's just for you to be able to get the visa." She was visiting on a business trip, and someone who knew the predicament I was in gave me her connection. I agreed with her conditions, and it became a done deal. She went back to the United States and sent over the documents I needed to present to the consulate at the American embassy in Lagos, Nigeria.

As I arrived at Newark Liberty International Airport that winter, in my green suit with no winter jacket, I looked at my watch and looked outside the airport. What I saw was a conflicting message, and this was due to the six-hour time difference between Nigeria and New Jersey. I wandered around the airport and took a couple of rides on the airport trains, as I enjoyed the beauty of the country before facing the reality of life.

I later took a taxi to Hackensack, trying to locate an address that turned out to be an office. It was in the middle of the night. After I had paid a hundred dollars to the taxi driver to take me back to the airport, he instead took me straight to a police station. Even though the police saw me as one who would definitely be a public charge to the country considering my circumstances, I had legal documents. They told the taxi driver to take me to a hotel. When we stepped out of the police station, I disclosed to the taxi driver that what I gave him was the only money I had; therefore, I needed him to take me back to the airport not a hotel.

The taxi driver at this point obediently took me back to the airport, where I continued my dangerous journey in a dangerous world. I stayed around until the freezing climate kept me from carrying my suitcase anymore. But I was able to put all the files I had inside of the suit I was wearing so as to cover my chest and stay a little warmer.

After I had succeeded in getting someone on the phone to come get me at the airport, he sent one of his workers to go pick me up.

When the messenger came, the airport employees announced my name everywhere, but I could not hear because my ears were frozen. So the messenger left, and I continued my stay in the airport area.

Many American women working at the airport approached me and volunteered to help me out, but I turned them down. What was I thinking? What was really behind my strong will to rough it out? I believe God has a reason for everything. I continued making calls to a man who actually came from my home town, whose number was given to me by a good friend of mine. I didn't know how to use those pay phones, but people were helping me with the calls.

When I got him on the phone again, he started yelling, "I sent someone to come get you, and you were nowhere to be found! They announced your name repeatedly, and you did not answer. Now tell me where you are, for I will come there myself for the very last time, and if I don't see you, forget it. Because I don't really care at this point! Don't you know that it is dangerous to go to America without proper arrangements? What if I traveled to Puerto Rico as I had anticipated? Do you know you can easily die of cold?" I had no choice but to patiently wait for him to finish telling me off—my concern was just to get out of the airport.

When he finally reached the airport, I had been in the United States two days and was almost a dead man. Of course, I was not able to lift my suitcase at that point. My fingers were all frozen. He took me home and gave me food, a shower, and clothes, before sending me out to the dangerous world the same day. He introduced me to someone who became my roommate. My coming-to-America experience went from the frying pan to the fire.

A couple of months after coming to America, I found myself out on the street and in the cold again. Guess what happened this time. Right after my roommate collected my share of the rent for our one-bedroom apartment building in Hackensack, New Jersey, we got evicted. I had so many questions, but whom could I ask? We ended up living in a car for a couple of weeks before we were able to get a studio apartment, still in Hackensack. Thank God I started working right after my arrival.

One day, I received a UPS delivery of exercise equipment, that actually bore my name on the package. When my roommate came back, I told him about the surprise delivery. Guess what he said? "Oh! I remember. I actually ordered this piece of equipment, but I put your name on it just in case I was not available during the delivery. That way you could receive it for me." As a newbie, I never imagined that he had used my personal information, obtained credit cards, and was buying things he needed and wanted. I found out when the credit card companies started calling me to pay my bills.

A check was sent to me from an airline company that lost my baggage during a trip; he collected it, forged my signature, and cashed it. I kept calling the company about my check. One day, they told me that the check had been delivered to me and had even been cashed. I asked, "Where was it cashed?" When they told me where, I recognized the location.

I had to move out of the studio apartment after I had noticed this bizarre incident from my roommate, but my conviction and strength to move did not come until I met one Timothy Aghaji at the FUBU warehouse facility in Secaucus, New Jersey. At the facility, I noticed someone staring at me. After a while, he came closer and asked, "*Nwokem, I bu onye ebee?*" He spoke my language! What it means is, "My friend, where are you from?" When I mentioned my town, he shouted because it so happened that we both came from the same local government area. I immediately narrated my roommate stories to Timothy, and he told me to run for my life. I ran and continued my journey into a dangerous world.

Timothy and I went ahead and got a two-bedroom apartment on Stuyvesant Avenue in Irvington, New Jersey. Today, Tim has moved on and is happily married, with many children. And I have come a long way in my journey, as I now live my quiet life in a quiet side of the country. Thank God I met Tim.

It Could Be Worse

After I had finished telling my own story, I realized that there are even worse situations out there. I traveled to the United States by air, but some people actually crossed the border by land on foot. Some immigrants from Mexico spend their life savings only to die in the desert in an attempt to cross into the United States. All they go with is hope, and hope can only go so far. When you have lost all the nutrients and electrolytes in your body, the body starts shutting down.

Sometimes I wonder, "Do American-born citizens actually know what others go through in order to come to America?" Apparently, some of them don't; the way they take what they have for granted says it all. Many people think the government owes them, and for that they sit and demand welfare while indulging in all kinds of atrocities. And when they see an African immigrant doing well in school or in a career, they get jealous. They say that the Africans came here to take away the resources that belong to them. How can it belong to you when you don't want to grab it? Schools are there for you, but you deliberately chose to be illiterate. In countries where people have to pay tuition to be able to go to school, people are doing it, regardless; but in America, where you have free education to an extent, many still don't have a high school diploma.

I implore you to look around and start counting your blessings before it's too late. Appreciate what you have and aspire for greatness, notwithstanding how dangerous the world is.

The Power beyond Physicality

When you have made an adventurous trip to a foreign land far from home, out of desperation or eagerness to focus, you tend to ignore the spirit of fear in situations that are supposed to be scary. Within my first few months in the United States, I noticed that whenever I found myself in danger, one particular man would come to my rescue. When I was stranded somewhere and had no ride home, this guy would show up. When it was really cold, and I had to walk to work from Hackensack to River Edge wearing only a windbreaker (as a new immigrant who couldn't afford heavy jackets yet), he would appear with his Nissan Altima to give me a ride. He kept appearing and continued to help me until one day I decided to break the silence. I asked him, "What is your name?"

He answered, "Wale."

"Who are you?" I asked.

"I am a Nigerian, but I came from London."

I told this skinny, dark-skinned, kind-hearted gentleman that he looked exactly like my late brother, Nwachukwu.

He paused, stared at me, and said, "Well, people can really look alike."

"Wale" later disappeared into the world (though after completing his mission), and I can tell you never to underestimate the power beyond physicality. Many things happen for a reason. When you think that you are alone, that's when God proves that you are not. When it looks like all hope is lost, that's when he brings a comforter. I have seen and witnessed power beyond the ordinary.

Back in the days when I was still in New Jersey, I was pulled over by a New York trooper for speeding while I was on my way to Rhode Island, and I was greeted with multiple tickets. The cop told me that he would give me a couple of tickets. In my understanding, a couple should be two, right? This police officer gave me *four* tickets. Out of the four, one was supposed to carry a lot more weight than the rest. I basically didn't have valid car insurance. Car insurance in New Jersey is the most expensive in the United States, but that's not an excuse. I talked to one of my professors who was an attorney. She said, "So you basically didn't provide any insurance when you got pulled over, right?"

I replied, "I gave him a bogus one."

She furiously told me to get ready for jail.

I went home to my one-bedroom apartment and realized that crying would not help me. My mother and father, who were far away in Africa, would not help me either. Guess what I did? Out of God's inspiration, I decided to use salt to wash my hands while I cried out to the Lord. I did that with faith. As my court date was fast approaching, I received a letter, signed by the New York State commissioner of police that my case had been dismissed. What else can I tell you? There is more to the world than what we see.

Will Smith's movie *The Pursuit of Happyness* reminds me so much of what I went through in America in my effort to make ends meet. I melted watching it because Will is a true character and watching him tells a lot about perseverance and optimism. You can never go wrong by believing in yourself and your ability to succeed, notwithstanding the huddles on the way. Many obstacles could have prevented Will from continuing his pursuit, but he never gave up.

Even when he was faced with the danger of losing his apartment, danger of getting killed by a car, and even danger of missing a job interview due to an unforeseen circumstance, Will did not succumb to the fear of failure. In him, I was inspired.

I remember those days: I would go to school and come back home with a bunch of parking tickets. There was no amount of caution that really helped me avoid tickets in New Jersey.

I parked my car for three minutes to grab something in a store; by the time I came back, I had already been ticketed. I woke up very early one Monday morning to move my car from the sweeping side; by the time I got there, it was already ticketed. I said to myself, "Okay, let it stay since it has been ticketed already." I went back upstairs and prepared for school. By the time I came back downstairs to go to school, it had already been towed.

One day I went to Brooklyn to visit Emeka Abuadinma, and I parked my car on the street. When I came out to go home, the police officers had given me a ticket in addition to the one I got on my way to Brooklyn for a bad left brake light. I went home with two tickets that day. It couldn't be any more frustrating.

On another regular day, I dropped a friend's sister at the airport and helped her with her luggage. When I returned to drive off, I found out that my car had been towed. All these might sound like tall tales, but I couldn't be more truthful. Some true stories are more easily experienced than told. Whoever has not been through the struggles and pursuit of happiness will not comprehend Will Smith's *Pursuit of Happyness*.

Life is good, but you have to overlook the dangerous aspect of it to maintain a memorable diary. Life is indeed a journey.

The Magic Number

Despite the dangers, struggles, and trials of life, an optimistic person will always come out a winner. When it looked like nothing was making sense for me, everything turned around like magic. That year, I got married, my wife had our first child, I graduated from university, and I became a United States citizen. All this happened the same year! Twenty-nine was indeed the magic number for me—no doubt about that. Friends and well-wishers came together at my apartment and celebrated with me. Because I did not plan these things and they happened the way they did, I am convinced that when the appointed time comes, no man or devil can stop you from grabbing your blessings.

Life changed for me totally that year; from a youngster to a father, from an undergraduate to a graduate. I began to face a new phase of life—one that changed my perceptions. I began to realize the importance of family. I began to worry about how to provide for my family and how to raise my child to be the best she could be. I began to weigh my actions before embarking on any risky or dangerous activities. I began to worry more about what would happen to my family if something happened to me. I felt an automatic presence of more responsibility —the innate sense that tells me when to make a trip and when to say no, when to say something and when to shut up, and even when to draw the line between my African mentality and American culture, especially toward my wife.

My prayer is for everyone to discover their magic number because your magic number can unlock the windows of life and take you to a desirable destination. I will never regret the year I turned twenty-nine because that was when every life-changing event happened.

Points to Ponder

1. A journey is dangerous when you don't know where you are going and what to expect along the way.

2. A journey is even more—in fact, extremely—dangerous if you are walking across the border in search of greener pastures. What is so green in America that you cannot find it in Africa and South America? Is it worth it to embark on a journey that you know within yourself is too dangerous?

3. When one door closes, another one opens. When a hometown man refused to sign an affidavit of support for me, a stranger signed instead. America, here I am.

4. The roommate who took advantage of a newbie definitely paid the price for his actions.

5. Mind how you treat a new person because we don't know who will help each other tomorrow.

6. What goes around comes around.

7. God sent Timothy to go to a FUBU warehouse in Secaucus, New Jersey, just to rescue me from the hands of a wicked roommate.

8. There is absolutely nothing wrong with being an adventurer, but you have to be brave so you can withstand the challenges that come with it.

9. If only the American-born citizens knew what immigrants go through to come and survive here, they would appreciate what they have.

CHAPTER 5

BETRAYAL IN FRIENDSHIPS

Nweke, a very intelligent Nigerian, was capable of being an attorney but, due to some troubles in life, found it difficult to keep his head up or make ends meet. Whoever saw him noticed right away that he had something special in him, yet he worked as nothing more than a security guard. He became bitter whenever he realized his potential was still very far from materializing. He enrolled in colleges and had the highest of grades but still could not graduate because something would always happen along the line.

He spoke like a law professor but could not get a degree after trying numerous colleges. Most immigrants drive in New Jersey, but Nweke transferred constantly from one bus to another to go to his security jobs. Don't get me wrong: Nweke was a very hard-working Nigerian.

He visited his friend Uche from time to time, but never allowed Uche to visit him back. When he needed to go to shopping, he would call on Uche for a ride, and Uche would show up right away.

One day he needed to take an aunt to JFK Airport in New York, and he called on Uche. Uche came to Hackensack and picked them both up and headed to the airport. Right before Verrazano Bridge, there was a very heavy traffic jam—bumper to bumper. The aunt became rude to Uche because she thought she was going to miss her flight. Clearly, though, Uche was not the cause of the traffic.

At the bridge, Uche asked Nweke for the toll fee, but Nweke was broke as usual. Tension was high in the car. Uche was just the victim of circumstances. First of all, he was not getting paid for the taxi service he was rendering—it was just a favor for his friend, who did not want to pay even the toll. Second, the aunt did not want to leave him alone to drive because she thought he was driving too slowly.

On their way back to New Jersey, after they had dropped off the disgruntled and ungrateful aunt, Nweke told Uche to take Brooklyn Bridge. The only reason for that was so he could avoid being asked again for toll money. Uche said, "No way! I am not taking Brooklyn Bridge. First of all, there is too much traffic there. Second, I don't have the patience for that many cars and people in New York City. Moreover, I don't want to hit anyone."

They got to Verrazano Bridge again, and Nweke didn't even wait to be asked for money before he said, "I don't have money. You already know my problems." Uche paid again and they crossed into New Jersey. At this point Uche was becoming furious.

Nweke on a different day had introduced Uche to a local fast-food restaurant, where they usually go eat "Italian cheeseburgers" on Springfield Avenue in Irvington. Of course they were both bachelors, but whenever they got there Uche would pay for both of them. At some point, Uche began to ask himself, "Does it mean that this young man really doesn't have money? He never has money, and we do the same security job. He is always complaining about money. Or maybe he is just playing smart." Uche's mentality is that one good turn deserves another. But Nweke doesn't believe in that. So Uche started to question the friendship, which obviously did not yield any reciprocity. Uche was always giving—his money, his time, and even his car—just to please his friend. "No, things are not right. This friendship is so one-sided." Uche woke up from his slumber and cautioned himself against continuing the relationship as it was.

One day, Nweke needed to borrow Microsoft software and told Uche that he would come on Friday evening for it. On Friday evening Nweke came knocking at the door, but Uche decided not to open the door for his "friend." Uche had decided that enough was enough. "If you think I am a fool, well you can go and enjoy my past foolishness, because I can't continue a friendship that is so parasitic in nature," he thought. When Nweke got tired of knocking and pacing, he left.

When they next saw each other, Nweke asked him what had happened. He replied, "Sorry, I went out."

Nweke said, "But I saw your car."

He replied, "Someone picked me up." They moved on.

It was a cold Sunday night one winter when Nweke and Uche went to a security job in Hillside, New Jersey. Maytag was the facility where washing machines are manufactured and stacked for distribution to retailers. The security guards usually take turns sleeping while on duty. This is so that if someone comes, one person will wake the other person up. But this time, they arrived at work in their heavy woolen jackets, turned on their portable heater, and both went to sleep at the same time. When a Maytag employee came around, he found out that both guards were passed out. He woke them up. Uche was really mad at Nweke for falling asleep instead of waiting for his turn.

Nweke promised to stay awake and wait for his turn this time. Uche went to sleep, and a supervisor came for a field inspection. Guess what Nweke did? He quietly opened the door for the supervisor to come in and catch his friend, Uche, sleeping. Uche was written up and eventually got fired for sleeping on duty. And that was the end of Uche's job at SOS security services.

His friend, whom he had done everything for, let him down and got him fired. As Sherrilyn Kenyon said, "Everyone suffers at least one bad betrayal in their lifetime. It's what unites us. The trick is not to let it destroy your trust in others when that happens. Don't let them take that from you."

American Visa

One particular Nigerian number that I was not familiar with kept calling me. One fateful day, I decided to answer the call, considering how persistent the caller had been. It was a former schoolmate, who obviously needed something.

"Hello, Tochukwu. How are you? This is Ikenna calling you from Lagos."

"Wow! Will wonders never cease? Where have you been, Ikenna?"

He replied, "I have been here in Lagos doing my business."

"What business?"

"I sell caterpillar parts," he said.

"Well, I'm glad you are doing well," I congratulated him.

Then he came up with his request. He asked me to please send him an invitation letter so he could come and buy some caterpillar parts in the United States. He also asked me to search for a reputable company he could deal with. I was interested. Other people would call for money, but he called for an opportunity to take his business to the next level. Nothing wrong with that, I thought. Any opportunity for advancement should not be discouraged.

I searched around and was able to get him a company in New Jersey. He started telling me how he had been traveling to France, Italy, the United Kingdom, and so forth.

I was truly impressed and convinced that he was into some great business, but I had no clue whatsoever that it also could be something not genuine. I just couldn't look beyond the facade. I said, "Hey, it is really nice speaking with you, but I'm sorry. I can't just provide my documents to you."

At this point, he spoke up more firmly. "Listen, I am a very successful businessman and you are free to ask anyone. I just need your help. Don't give me money. What I need is just the papers to be able to get the visa to the United States. I will do my business and go back to Nigeria. You have nothing to worry about and absolutely nothing to lose."

I said, "Okay, why not?" Why should I even try to hinder someone from getting an opportunity to come to America? My fear basically was that he might come and decide not to go back, and it would be on me. But he convinced me of how comfortable he was, and, honestly, anyone who is financially comfortable in Nigeria doesn't need to come live here. So on that note, I made up my mind to do it.

I sent the documents. He went to the American embassy in Victoria Island, Lagos, and was issued a two-year-multiple visa. He called me and said thank you. That's all I got and I had no problem with that. Now he has the visa and he will come at his convenient time.

I made a trip to Nigeria. As I was enjoying the nightlife in Abuja with my cousin, my friends, and a pan of gizzards, I remembered Ikenna. I knew he lived in Lagos not Abuja, but I called him just to chat him up and let him know that I was in the country since I didn't know when he wanted to make his trip to the United States. When he answered me, I told him that I was in Abuja. Coincidentally, he told me he had just checked into one of the hotels in Abuja. He asked me where I was; I gave the phone to my friend Marvin to explain to him. After that, he said, "I will see you in ten minutes." He came over and we all spent what was supposed to be a memorable time together after many years apart.

After a couple of weeks, my phone rang and it was Ikenna. "Where are you?" he asked. I replied I was at Murtala Muhammed International Airport, getting ready to leave the country. He said, "Okay, I will see you in the US. I'm heading to London, and from there I will come to *Yankee*."

I boarded an aircraft to fly back to the United States. As I got to O'Hare International Airport in Chicago, I was told to step aside. The customs and some federal government special agents surrounded me and ransacked my luggage. Even though they did not find anything, they were not satisfied. They pulled me into a small room and made me sit and wait for a very long time while they were monitoring me through their camera.

When it became necessary, I asked for permission to use the restroom. Instead of letting me go, they escorted me to the bathroom. That was when I realized that something was definitely up. I began to pray, even though I didn't do anything, but I know the devil can do anything. I pulled out my cellular phone to call my wife so she could start praying; they took my phone away from me.

After sitting for a very long time, they asked me if I needed to drink anything and I answered no. That was when they began a thorough interrogation. My connecting flight was already gone, but that wasn't the issue at this point.

"What do you do for a living? Where are you coming from? Why did you travel? Where and when did you visit? What is your level of education? Why do you travel so frequently because I noticed you have been to Germany a number of times. You have been to the Netherlands, London, France, and have visited Nigeria multiple times within a short period of time? How much do you make? What was the last phone call you made before leaving Nigeria? Who is Ikenna and when was the last time you saw him or spoke with him?"

I complied with all the orders and innocently answered all the questions to the best of my knowledge. They took my wallet from me and copied everything in it. They stripped me down and asked me why I didn't want to take water. I told them, "You know what? Give me food and water together, and I will eat and drink as much as you want. Because I have realized there is a serious problem."

At this point they concentrated more on Ikenna. "When did you know Ikenna, and where is he? I told them that Ikenna was a schoolmate—a friend who needed to come here for business and I had sent him an invitation letter. I told them when we spoke last and how we saw each other in Abuja. They opened up the can of worms at this juncture by saying, "Do you know that Ikenna is a drug dealer? Right now, as we speak, he is being held at the airport in Philadelphia for smuggling one of the largest amounts of heroin onto US soil through swallowing. Therefore, we have the right to arrest you for being part of the plan. You conspired with and sponsored an international drug dealer with the intent to harbor him. You now have the right to remain silent because anything you say can be used against you."

Considering that I had been in the airport with them for the whole day without any sign of reaction to illicit drugs in my belly, they didn't see any reason to still take me to a hospital for an X-ray as they had threatened earlier. But as they threatened to arrest me for charges other than possession of illegal drugs, I stated, "You folks are doing such a wonderful job, and I commend you for that. But in this case, gentlemen, there is absolutely no probable cause to arrest me. Ikenna was headed east and I was headed west. There was no plan of meeting up in Jersey as he told you. My flight itinerary says it all. Therefore, I plead with you to let go of an innocent man, who was only showing kindness to humanity. It is true I know him. I sent him the invitation letter. I also met with him in my trip, and I even spoke with him right before I boarded, but in this situation, these circumstantial evidences you have are mere coincidence to the detriment of my justice and are not tangible enough to get me arrested for a crime I did not commit."

I was let go pending on continued investigations. I was a "happy camper," to be sure. I went home rejoicing and giving testimony. What happened next? My MoneyGram account was broken into in order to monitor my international monetary transactions. I was notified by MoneyGram of the new development, but what choice do I have? Privacy is gone, but I'm alive and free.

I will never encourage you to give up on humanity, but in your attempt to help others, just don't be like me because the consequences in your case might be different. According to Ralph Waldo Emerson, "Life is a succession of lessons which must be lived to be understood" Be wise!

Points to Ponder

1. Friendships are not supposed to be one-sided. When they are, something is wrong.
2. Try not to take advantage of your friend. He might look foolish, but one day, he will wake up and put you in your place.
3. Nweke was a very intelligent man who couldn't figure out why he couldn't climb higher than a security job despite his intellectual capabilities.
4. Nweke betrayed his friend Uche by letting him get caught and fired by their SOS supervisor for sleeping on duty.
5. Friends who use you without ever returning a favor will also be willing to betray you.
6. Don't sleep on duty.
7. Don't let your kindness lead you into trouble.
8. Beware of bad friends.
9. Choose your friends and don't let them choose you.
10. Friendship is not by force. If it doesn't work out, move on with your dignity.

CHAPTER 6

ADAPTABILITY TO CHANGE

Change is definitely the most constant thing in life; therefore, I strongly believe that we cannot do well without changing our attitudes, jobs, clothes, houses, states, business, level of education, and so on.

In other words, "adaptability to change" in this context is the ability to respond to a positive stimulus or incentive. We do that by first of all ascertaining that the change we about to embark on is a positive one (of good course). A flexible person, for example, is more capable of adjusting to a new or different way of life. You adapt when you can fit in and survive, notwithstanding being in a different environment or culture.

On a very cold winter morning in Newark, New Jersey, I woke up to go to school, looked out the window, and saw only heaps of snow covering everything. My ever-clean Nissan Sentra was buried by the snowplow. I automatically became lazy. I was just too tired to go shovel the snow and clean the driveway in order to get out. I was already getting tired of the cold temperature and messy debris. As I was contemplating what to do with the car, the snow, the coldness, and all that, my cellular phone rang. Lo and behold it was Prince Festus—we went to college together at NJCU. My first question was, "Prince, where did you say you moved to?"

"Oh, I relocated to Arizona," Prince answered.

I asked him, "Is it cold over there?"

He said, "No, Arizona is the place to be."

I asked him again, "Does it snow there?"

He replied, "Not at all."

I then asked myself, "What are you still doing here?"

I made a very quick decision to embrace change.

I decided to visit Prince in Arizona, and when I got there, I fell in love with the state. I found in Arizona a clean environment. It was an easy-going, slow-paced state, with a warm climate and, most importantly, a less congested population. Who would not leave a densely populated New Jersey for this beautiful atmosphere?

Agent of Change

In Prince, I found an agent of change—no doubt. He and his family let us in, and my wife, daughter, and I all moved into his apartment that summer. He was indeed the agent used to bring a change of environment to my life. Maybe I would have died of cold if I didn't make that move! Who knows?

If you do not create change, change will create you. People came to my wife and told her to discourage me from moving from New Jersey, but that didn't matter because it was about what was good for us, not friends. Because I was the drummer for the Igbo Anglican Church, it was also hard for them to let me go, but they had no power to restrict me. After their effort to talk me out of moving proved fruitless, they prayed for us and set us free.

Our next-door neighbors weren't pleased either. The couple stopped talking to us. The man saw me carrying heavy boxes downstairs, but he ignored me and allowed me to suffer alone. Later, they came to my Arizona residence on a vacation, and that was when they apologized to us. They confessed that they did what they did because they were afraid to lose us as neighbors and family friends.

My ability to respond to the stimulus of change reunited us once again and even gave them a vacation home in Arizona.

Don't get me wrong. Change can be scary, but it definitely gives you strength, progress, opportunities, and new beginnings. As George Bernard Shaw said, "Progress is impossible without change, and those who cannot change their minds cannot change anything."

In today's world of ingratitude, it might be hard to find someone testifying about how his neighbor changed his life, but do not stop being the agent of change. You are not doing it for men to praise you but for lives to be changed. Sometimes change might require giving up one's life like Martin Luther King Jr. did. Dr. King changed the world with words. He stopped segregation. He traveled state to state giving speeches about peace and kindness.

I believe that anyone can be an agent of change in little ways. There is absolutely no limit to how you can influence another person's life. Therefore, if you have the opportunity to bring positive social change to individuals, groups, or society, please, by all means, do it.

I will never stop praising teachers for what they do year in and year out. They change the economy of our nation by imparting knowledge and skills to students, which help them acquire jobs. They nurture the future generation of politicians, public servants, legal and medical professionals, and so on.

I have heard people ask me, "Why are you not working at such-and-such place?" My answer was "someone has to be an agent of change in the corrections environment." There's got to be a way to reshape the mentality of people in prison. Also there should be a way to help the inmates become better individuals regardless of prison status or stigma. As a matter of fact, I try not to dwell on their offenses. I read a lot and I see a lot, but I don't use what I have read about one particular inmate to judge him. I try to give them equal chances to succeed.

To that end, we implement what we call a "parallel universe" in prison. In today's correctional practices, we give inmates the opportunity to participate in some positive activities that can help change their lives while still incarcerated. Inmates go to school in prison, they go to church, and they learn new skills and are allowed to work while incarcerated. They also get paid every two weeks just like regular people outside, but only those who can participate in the programs. They engage in real-life activities while serving time. They are basically given the chance to change. That's what we mean by "parallel universe."

We derive pleasure from spreading change through the administering of various programs like cognitive thinking for a change, reentry programs, parenting classes, domestic violence awareness programs, conflict resolution, cultural diversity, and money management. We provide different programs that not only keep inmates busy while serving time but also change their perspectives. Through such programming, inmates tend to realize that there are so many productive things to do while in prison and when released from prison. They look forward to making use of the skills they acquired in prison. They also get the opportunity to get a job with the education they obtained while serving time. Most inmates who complete a sex offender education and treatment program (SOETP) are able to abstain from things that can lead them into engaging in future sexual offenses. In fact, some of the inmates realize their full potential by the time they are done serving time.

We develop and maintain a collaborative support system for an offender, and work together with family members and in cooperation with social service agencies and community organizations so that the offender is able to access relevant support services while in prison and after he or she is released. This helps ensure successful reintegration into the community. We basically help offenders prepare for a successful entry back into society once they have completed their prison sentences.

In prison, inmates battle with psychological reminders that they are incarcerated and have lost touch with the world and therefore can never become anything good again in their lives. They need people to tell them to turn a deaf ear to what they hear. If an inmate complains to another inmate, like a next-door neighbor, about what he is going through, that inmate will sometimes pass a robe from his cell and tell him to kill himself. I am not kidding: they literarily aid the suicide of other inmates.

But overall, adapting to change puts one on a different level of advancement. Therefore, your decision to embrace change is what separates you from stagnation. Many people are afraid of the danger they will face when they change what they are already used to, because they forget to look beyond just the limitations.

Points to Ponder

1. Anyone can be an agent of change; just invent your own little way of affecting people in a positive way.

2. Be flexible as a person and be accommodating as a child of God.

3. Some of your positive ways of helping people out might be interpreted as weakness, but ignore that and keep up the good work.

4. If you have to relocate to another state for your own health and for the good of the family, take responsibility and do it.

5. Dr. King traveled from state to state speaking of peace. He changed many things in the United States, and segregation is one of them.

6. Embrace change even when it is not convenient.

7. You can listen, but don't take people's bad advice when it comes to making a good decision for your family.

8. Adapting to change puts one on a different level of advancement.

CHAPTER 7

DOING PRISON TIME

Prison is a world of its own. It's a place where everything happens; incarcerated offenders have the right to be corrected or institutionalized. When you choose to be corrected, you do your time and move on with your life, but when you decide to be institutionalized, you just get accustomed to the system and recycle within. The more acculturated you become, the harder it is to want to be released.

It's sad but it's true that some people don't want to be released from prison, either because they have burnt their bridges and have nowhere else to go or because they have lost their coping mechanism. "Coping mechanism" in this context is the drive to independently survive outside of prison walls.

Who would ever imagine working in a prison? And who would ever have the dream of working with criminals? While we're at it, who are the criminals? Criminals are those who have been found guilty of committing offenses (crimes). In other words, one is not considered a criminal until it is proven beyond reasonable doubt in a court of law that one is guilty of a crime.

Experience has made me realize that some careers you embark on because you have to do something, some you start because you actually have a passion for them, but some are done out of necessity. Considering how important it is to protect the community by keeping convicted felons incarcerated, having a desire to work for the Arizona Department of Corrections, where there are many interesting individuals, should never go unrecognized. In this I see a mark of bravery, doing what the majority would not want to do under normal circumstances.

In the end, the survivors of prison, whether as a prisoner or as an employee can say it's the survival of the fittest. Nevertheless, it's not really as treacherous as people perceive it. I know it takes guts to work in prison, but it also takes courage and determination to be an adult.

Moreover, some workers or inmates get in alive and leave dead. Many people enter sane and leave insane. You witness and hear of staff assault here and there, and the big employees have been assaulted or even killed, as well as the small people.

A good question is how have I **survived**. Have I survived because I have been wiser than others or because I have been tougher? "Except the Lord build the house, they labor in vain that build it" (Psalm 127 KJV).

The correctional professionals basically do time with the inmates, with the difference of having the option of going home at the end of the shift. Other than that, it feels just the same. That's why I usually see it as everyone is "doing prison time."

Staff get depressed and face other mental challenges because of what they go through working in a prison. They see deaths, bloody assaults, and different kinds of suicide incidents as well as executions (intentional killing of death-row inmates with the use of lethal injections) in some states. They hear the ranting and chanting of inmates with various mental problems; some inmates seem capable of keeping your ears buzzing and your head pounding the whole night. It can be traumatic working in a prison because you are emotionally drained and physically exhausted.

Cases of depression among staff have been an area of concern. A captain once took his bike into the desert in Florence, Arizona, and shot and killed himself. A main control officer shot and killed himself while on post. My academy classmate, who used to sit right next to me, one day shot and killed himself as a result of Department of Corrections work-related depression and frustration. This is to mention but a few. You work in an environment surrounded by negative thoughts. Some officers have even claimed seeing or hearing ghosts in prisons.

Has it been a challenging career so far? Yes, it has—but an interesting one indeed. It's a career where even some coworkers (the ones who have eyes but cannot see) see you as one who does not fit in, a career where some individuals feel superior to others. It's also a career in which I have learned to prove them wrong, and I have proved them wrong by standing out. I have proved them wrong by excelling in what I do.

It might surprise you to hear the extent of prejudice—that even an inmate once told me, "I will send you back to Africa where you belong so you can run around with animals—I know that's what you do."

Many inmates want everything to go their way. They are the most manipulative set of individuals on earth and will never give up playing their games. They play mind games with you, especially if you are new. Many of them think they are entitled to everything, and they take it out on you. Some of them are smarter than the workers. There are too many talented professionals who are incarcerated just because of some bad choices; talent and resources are being wasted in prisons. They know all the federal and state laws, which they use to tell you what they are entitled to.

My philosophy is to treat all inmates with fairness and equality but without any fear or favor. In other words, I don't indulge in preferential treatment. Rather, I will be fair, firm, and consistent.

In the end, the DOC job is one where I feel delighted to have influenced many lives by sharing positivity, knowledge, and inspiration with people. Despite the downsides, I cannot wish for a better career than this, which gives me the opportunity to bring hope to the hopeless. Correcting, counseling, rehabilitating, managing, protecting, changing, and releasing inmates as well as promoting moral values and principles in the prison environment make me feel accomplished.

What do you cherish doing in this dangerous world? Do you kick back and relax with the excuse of how dangerous it is out there? Don't get me wrong: it *is* a very dangerous world, but it's important for us to learn how to swim in that turbulent water instead of avoiding it entirely.

Behind the prison walls, inmates are further classified. There are minimum custody, medium custody, close custody, and maximum custody levels. The minimum yard consists of inmates with lesser charges (low-risk inmates), people convicted of nonviolent crimes. On the other hand, maximum custody is a lockdown, previously known as level 5, where the most dangerous criminals are incarcerated. Maximum custody is run by a special management unit (SMU), which requires special training and more caution. Minimum and medium custody prisons are open yards, where inmates are allowed to enjoy a little bit of freedom, but it is important not to mix sex offenders (SO) with the general population (GP). If such a mistake happens, someone could die for it. GP inmates tend to think that the SO inmates don't deserve to live, considering their atrocities. This makes me wonder how the pot can call the kettle black. One of the jobs of prison officials is to make sure no one dies, whether by suicide or murder. The goal is to make sure they do their time while becoming better individuals in society. But this is not always the result. You can only do your best and apply the best correctional practices so as to ensure safety for the public, staff, and inmates.

Correctional officers are responsible adults with a great sense of accountability. The lives of inmates are in the hands of the officers, for the most part, and sometimes, despite how careful they are, officers still find themselves in serious trouble.

This Is How It Happened

After the tedious nine-week-long academy training, what I wanted was to just go to work and enjoy my first government job. But what you want is not always what is needed of you. I was told to report to the special management unit II (SMU II). That's a level 5, maximum custody unit popularly known as the "super-max unit." The unit requires special skills, intense training, and extra carefulness.

I walked in the prison, trying to seem like a tough old-timer officer (super cop) but very scared inside. I was shocked to hear hardcore criminals inside their one-man cell call me "fish." In prison language, a fish is a newbie. I thought, "Oh my God, how do they know that I am new?" Of course they had been around long enough to tell when someone was a brand-new worker.

Work was full of one scary incident after another, but this is the climax: During my first year with the Department of Corrections (DOC), I was involved in a serious administrative investigation that had to do with the tragic death of one of the inmates under my custody. As one who was still on the one-year probation, I needed to be at my best to move on to the next phase of my correctional career. But as man proposes, God disposes. Correctional officers are "covered," meaning one can't just wake up and get you fired because he or she doesn't like you. There is a formal process for looking into whatever they think you did, and there are stages of administrative reviews before anyone can conclude that what you did is proven and that you have to be let go. In other words, firing someone in this job is like having a camel pass through the eye of a needle—except when you are still on probation. You can be fired easily if you have not finished your probation.

I was working in a control room at the SMU II when my floor officer came to me and shouted that I should activate ICS (incident command system). I asked, "What happened?"

Sounding scared, he replied, "An inmate is hanging!"

I told him to go ahead and activate *immediately*. Even though he was shaking, he picked up his radio and activated ICS. Then came the response team comprising officers, supervisors, cameras, and medical staff. I electronically opened the entrance door to the cluster as well as the pod door.

Because it's a maximum security unit, extra caution always has to be applied. As the response team got mentally and physically ready to rush into the cell for a possible rescue, I was instructed by the team leader to go ahead and open the cell door. I clicked the button on my computer, and the cell door opened. The inmate was taken down and CPR was administered right away but to no avail. All the mouth-to-mouth and chest compression did not change the fact that the inmate had turned blue before he was discovered by my floor officer.

When the 11:00 a.m. formal count was conducted by this floor officer, the inmate was already hanging dead. However, the inmate was counted in as living and breathing, and the count was cleared with no discrepancies. What went wrong and when? I would rather leave the question for another day. As humans, we can never run away from misfortunes, but we should always be ready to push through.

In lockdowns, you are expected to conduct a security check once every thirty minutes to avoid things like this happening. Doing the job correctly requires climbing up and down the stairs almost nonstop for the entire shift. We were doing twelve-hour shifts at the time. Good luck with those walks!

During feeding, you climb the stairs while holding a stack of trays. You feed them, pick up trays, pass out toilet paper and shavers, conduct recreation turns, and still maintain health and welfare checks. In the process of recreation turns, you have to apply the best protective security measures while using your handcuffs so as to avoid mistakes. Any mistakes could result in staff assault. Some inmates are skillful at slipping their arms off the handcuffs. That's why it's important to put them on correctly and always double-lock the cuffs. If, through your carelessness, an inmate grabs your cuffs or your hands and hurts you badly, you will still get in trouble for not following proper procedures.

You might be the best worker but still pray that nothing bad happens along the line because you will go through hell on earth. In my case, the worst had happened—the hanging. And that was the beginning of my hard times in this mentally and physically draining work environment. As I was still trying to record everything that happened, my log book was grabbed by a supervisor. This is because they didn't want to give me any opportunity to add, change, or fix anything—they don't want you to alter a legal document. Doing so could obstruct or influence the outcome of their investigation.

Even though I survived the six months of investigation that saw my floor officer let go, I was left with nothing but despair throughout the investigation. I was moved from the unit to a temporary work assignment (TWA) for the duration, with nothing much to show for it. I was isolated and dejected about being regarded by people as an inmate killer. Many officers told me what they had overheard. One said, "I heard from one of the top union representatives that you would be fired. I am not telling you to scare you but for you to look for something else ahead of time because you have a young family to support." I told her that I would trust God.

Coincidentally, I answered a telephone call one day during the investigation and heard, "I want to know what happened to my son." I thought, "Oh no! Oh my God! This is the wrong person to ask." She was, indeed, asking about the inmate in question. It looked like I couldn't run away from it.

When I looked around, all I saw was danger and worry. But my profound gratitude goes to Sergeant Ziebell and Deputy Warden Carl ToersBijns for standing by me throughout my trial period at DOC. These wonderful individuals believed I had a bright career ahead of me and wanted to give me a chance to prove my worth. Their efforts, combined with my ability to give a detailed and honest account of what happened on July 4, 2007, saw me come out "not guilty." When many had given up hope, these two individuals were optimistic about my victory. They encouraged me along as I walked through the dark tunnel.

At this super-max unit, you worry not only about the amount of work you have to deal with but also about inmates who do not want to continue existing, especially in that small cell, with one hour of recreation in twenty-four hours.

You are always on your feet, climbing stairs more often than you can count over the course of a twelve-hour shift. You wear a heavy vest, with all the protective inserts, as you sweat like a roasting goat. If you fail to drink enough water, you get dehydrated and will be taken to the hospital.

Life is tough for lockdown inmates; how much more so for the officers? These inmates will make life as close to miserable for the officers as possible. In fact, miserable might seem like an understatement. Majority of them have accepted life the way it is, with no vision or ambition. Most of them there have nothing to lose. They throw feces, urine, dart, or saliva at officers. The crazy ones will yell all day long. By the time you finish your shift for the day, you have a severe headache.

Of course, there are additional dangers. "Shanks" are prison-made weapons. Inmates make them and hide them very well as they wait for an opportunity to use them on any unfortunate staff: librarians, teachers, physicians, dentists, nurses, correctional officers, chaplains, or administrators. When they assault you, they try to do it in such a way that you will not have any chance of survival. Inmates can convert basically anything into a shank, ranging from toilet paper to iron doors. They use their bare fingers to grind out pieces of iron from their doors. Don't ask me where they get their strength because certain things they do are beyond human comprehension.

The Effect of Solitary Confinement

It's quite interesting to learn how life is on the other side of the world. Most times, when life is all milk and honey for you, it makes you ignorant of what others experience on a daily basis, especially people behind bars. Having been exposed to life in this dangerous world for eight years, I stand in a better position to share knowledge of working in a correctional facility.

Many of us watch television shows and documentaries about prison breaks or lockdowns. That gives you a little bit of an idea of what I mean by "solitary confinement." Solitary confinement is generally referred to as "the prison within the prison." The cell is approximately eighty square feet.

Inmates in solitary confinement are there for different reasons: protective segregation, mental illness, validated security threat groups (STG), condemned to death row, or violence in prison, those who will commit murder in a heartbeat.

This is where you see inmates hitting their heads on the wall as if their heads were soccer balls. Correctional officers command them to stop hurting themselves. Usually the next action after giving direct orders to stop is to spray the inmate. When these people can't feel the pain of hard walls, how do you think they can feel the burning pain of pepper spray? Some of them have built up tolerance to it anyway, so it's just like a person getting used to fire.

When I started my correctional career in this kind of facility, it baffled me to see so many inmates that were crazy. I kept asking myself, "Does it mean that they actually prosecute these mentally incompetent individuals and sentence them to prison, even though they know they don't have the mental capabilities to defend their actions?" It got me worried for a little while before I learned the truth.

When you are confined in one little cell with just a toilet, a sink, and a bed twenty-three hours a day for twenty-five years of your life, it would take the grace of God for you not to go crazy. Researchers have found little to suggest that extreme isolation is good for the psyche.

In one notorious study from the 1950s, University of Wisconsin psychologist Harry Harlow placed rhesus monkeys inside a custom-designed solitary chamber nicknamed "the pit of despair." Shaped like an inverted pyramid, the chamber had slippery sides that made climbing out all but impossible. After a day or two, Harlow wrote, "most subjects typically assume a hunched position in a corner of the bottom of the apparatus. One might presume at this point that they find their situation to be hopeless."

Harlow also found that monkeys kept in isolation ended up "profoundly disturbed, given to staring blankly and rocking in place for long periods, circling their cages repetitively, and mutilating themselves." Most readjusted eventually but not those that had been caged the longest. "Twelve months of isolation almost obliterated the animals socially," Harlow found.

A similar example of what solitary confinement can do to a living organism is this: I went to work one day and when I came back, my mother told me that she had caught a bird. We already had a cage, so she put this wild bird in a cage and fed her really well. After just three days, the wild bird stopped eating and hopping around. It was time to let her out; otherwise, she would die from being confined.

Another study was conducted in 1951 at McGill University, in which a group of graduate students were paid to stay in small chambers equipped with only a bed for an experiment on sensory deprivation. They could leave to use the bathroom, but that was all. They wore goggles and earphones to limit their sense of sight and hearing as well as gloves to limit their sense of touch. The plan was to observe students for six weeks, but not one lasted more than seven days. Nearly every student lost the ability "to think clearly about anything for any length of time" while several began to suffer hallucinations. "One man could see nothing but dogs," wrote one of the study collaborators, "another nothing but eyeglasses of various types, and so on."

In fact, in solitary confinement, inmates lose their minds and become more aggressive, violent, and suicidal. On one occasion, an inmate in confinement started drinking too much water just out of boredom. He kept drinking until it became a concern to the officers. As a matter of fact, he became intoxicated by consuming excessive amount of water. I didn't know that was possible until that night. As he was overwhelming his kidneys from drinking water, a correctional officer activated ICS. When the response team arrived, the inmate was commanded to stop, but he refused. He was then commanded to cuff up; he again refused. He got sprayed so he would stop, but he still refused. The team organized themselves and suited up for an immediate cell extraction. By the time they opened his cell and rushed in for a rescue, he had a ruptured rectum. He was taken to a health unit, where he was pronounced dead.

As we try to protect the public, staff, and other inmates from the dangerous activities of some inmates, a good number are losing their sanity and even their lives. So the Association of State Correctional Administrators (ASCA) have looked into the menace. There has got to be a way out of this mess because, even when they are released from prison, after too many years of solitary confinement, they cannot be any better. It's like releasing a wild animal onto the street. Inmates tend to demonstrate psychological and mental imbalance because they apparently gained no correction or rehabilitation whatsoever while serving time in solitary confinement.

So what's the point of having solitary confinement if it doesn't do the inmates any good or help society? My opinion is that managing the correctional population has created a dilemma: if you let them loose on the prison yard, you are running the risk of assault and other violent behaviors, and if you lock them down in solitary confinement, you increase their chances of going crazy. It's a bad hand.

Now, however, ASCA figures that the best approach is to introduce a step-down program. This is a good idea, but the consequences are yet to be determined. With the step-down program, the solitary inmates are given a little more freedom to participate in programs, on the hope that this will help them behave more like well-adjusted human beings. The intent is to bring them out a little more often and expose them to close-to-normal lifestyles. They are required to participate in a variety of programs and exhibit positive and acceptable behaviors. As they comply, they will be afforded progressively greater opportunities for recreation, work, programming, and out-of-cell time.

Whether this plan will cause more assaults in prison or will help the inmates act better, we don't know yet; however, a lack of sufficient staffing might hinder such an innovative idea. More correctional officers and program staff will be needed to withstand the challenges of this program.

Points to Ponder

1. Prison is an institution where everything happens. Some inmates get corrected and move on while some get institutionalized and recycle within.

2. The inmates who get rehabilitated take part in various correctional programs available to them.

3. The ones who get institutionalized decide they have little or nothing to lose. They might as well be the worst inmates they can be and assault as many staff as they can.

4. Life in prison can be depressing for inmates as well as the correctional professionals.

5. In prison, anything at all can be converted into a shank. For this reason, prison staff must work with extra caution.

6. Prison staff must always mind their surroundings and try not to take home the stress of work.

7. There are too many work-related suicides as a result of depression, high workloads, and high expectations. Seek counseling when needed.

8. Appreciate the people that helped you when you faced danger at work.

9. Learn how to swim in turbulent water instead of avoiding it entirely because almost everything we do in this world has a little bit of risk in it.

10. When life is all milk and honey, it is difficult to comprehend what people experience on the other side of the world.

11. Managing the correctional population has created a dilemma: If you let solitary confinement inmates loose on

the prison yard, you run the risk of more assaults. If you lock them in small cells alone, you increase their chances of going insane.

12. A step-down program has recently been introduced with high hopes that the innovative programming will improve the inmates' rehabilitation.

CHAPTER 8

CONGESTION IN PRISONS

Prisons are, for the most part, owned by the government: state and federal. But because too many people have chosen life in prison over life on the street, the management of prisons has escalated to private ownership too. Government facilities are not enough to house the ever-increasing number of offenders. Therefore, private investors jumped into the lucrative business of contracting out beds for our overcrowded state prison populations.

You can't blame these smart investors for their foresight. It's just like blaming a casket maker for joining the business of making caskets. The truth of the matter is that people will always die. So also, people will always go to prison, no matter how much the government tries. Whether it's government or private, prison is prison.

I found out one of the most frustrating parts of the job at the Arizona Department of Corrections is the issue of recidivism. Recidivism is measured by criminal acts that result in the rearrest, reconviction, or return to prison with or without a new sentence during a three-year period following the prisoner's release.

When you are working on an offender's release packet, you are excited that someone will get to go home and be reunited with family and friends, especially after so many years of incarceration. Little do you know that this particular offender is going to come back to prison, sooner rather than later. It kept troubling me until I got used to it. Don't allow yourself to get too excited and assume that you are releasing them for good and will not see them again. I used to think, "Oh yes, one less problem to worry about; he is going home." But guess what? It is just a continuous process because he isn't going very far. The inmates make this job one of the steadiest jobs on earth. Believe it or not, sometimes I wish they could all be released so we could just consider it done and all go home. But the reality remains that this is a twenty-four-hour business.

There are too many new offenders each day; meanwhile the old ones are just recycling as if prison is heaven. It's true some people are devastated finding themselves in prison due to one bad choice, but so many have found a home of sorts in prison. They can't survive elsewhere. Who takes responsibility for the high recidivism of inmates in American prisons? Is it the system, society, or parents? Let's delve deeper.

System

The criminal justice system is probably the most important of all the working systems in the United States. Since Americans keep the system busy, the system has developed methods to measure up to the demands of the people, especially the victims. We all demand justice for those wronged, and for justice to prevail, there should be a working system that includes of the following:

- Police
- Court
- Corrections

You can't discuss the criminal justice system without covering the aforementioned three entities.

The police are widely recognized as the entrance gate into the criminal justice system. When there is probable cause that an offense has been committed, it is the police that make the arrest. In any disturbance, guess who is the first responder? The police. Among the three entities the police probably have the most dangerous job to do. They face danger in responding to fights, domestic violence, shooting, kidnapping, rape, burglary, drug activities, murder cases, and more.

Prior to an arrest, the officer will read the Miranda rights, which state that the one arrested has the right to remain silent because anything said can be used in the court of law. After an arrest, the alleged offender prepares for court, with the knowledge that he or she is entitled to a lawyer.

Consider the complicated nature of the police job. Many times, victims are disappointed with the police if they believe that officers were too slow to arrive at a crime scene, didn't make an arrest as they wished, ignored their accusations, or failed to recover stolen property. It is always the police who stand between the victim and the perpetrator. As the perpetrator is fleeing from the police, the victim is running to the police to do something. Sometimes, the job of the police officers cannot get any more complicated.

It's such an unfortunate situation that many crimes are not solved. Some cases lack substantial evidence to prove that a crime has been committed while some are just too ambiguous. Are all parties always satisfied with the system? No, I don't think so.

The victim wants punishment for the perpetrator, treatment as the victim, and restitution (depending on the incident). Even though these things are not guaranteed, the system does not want to ignore the cry of the victims. Some of these victims go through emotional, physical, and psychological trauma as well as financial burden due to the incident. The system therefore takes punishment seriously, so as to minimize repetition and deter future crime. But before punishment is imposed on an individual, there has to be a trial. This is when the court comes in.

Court is considered a platform for the system. The judge presides over the court proceedings and allows for a free and fair trial. The alleged perpetrator is given the opportunity to be represented by an attorney, which is considered part of due process. Due process is intended to eliminate doubt and bias in a case as well as provide evidence that a case has been judged with all fairness. Due process also holds that the alleged perpetrator remains innocent until proven guilty in the court of law.

In court, you witness drama of all kinds. Victims don't like defense lawyers in any way. They believe defense lawyers are not on their side but are there to help the perpetrators. It's a little contradictory in the sense that an ordinary person would ask why anyone would want to defend someone who allegedly committed murder, rape, kidnapping, robbery, or some other crime. But we have to face the reality of life. And be aware that this system was developed on the idea that it prevents innocent people being sent to jail for crimes they didn't actually commit.

When a case goes against the perpetrator, the person faces punishment measurable to his or her offense(s). If the person is found guilty of a felony offense and is an adult, the offender goes straight to prison.

The corrections facility is basically the prison, and in the prison facility, it is a whole different ball game. Adult are told how to live. Their lives are controlled at this stage by the correctional officers. They are told what to do and when to do it. The goal is to keep offenders incarcerated until legally released, while they are being rehabilitated into changed and corrected individuals. Keeping offenders incarcerated keeps them away from their victims and protects the community from additional dangerous acts of such offenders.

The system cannot help but set a high expectation for the offenders even outside of prison. Just as the offenders are expected to do their time in prison, they are also expected to abide by the conditions of supervision once they're released on parole or probation. Many of these conditions are just too tough for them to meet. It can seem like the system sets former inmates up for failure with those difficult conditions, but how else can the system resolve the dilemma? This challenge increases the high return rate of offenders.

Inmates get released and they come back to prison after a couple of months. It is just too tough for them. Those conditions would be tough for anyone; therefore, the best approach is to stay away from the system from day one. This has become an epidemic. When you have history with the system, there is always that tendency of it reminding the law enforcement officers to check what you are up to.

Imagine being told that you can't have contact with your own child. This happens when your child is your victim or if you are convicted of child molestation. One of the conditions in the latter situation is that you can't have contact with minors. When you can't have contact with minors, you have been given a very difficult situation to handle. These are just a couple of examples of the conditions the system imposes on the offenders who have finished serving their time in prison. Let's be wise about the decisions we make.

Society

In society, in our beloved America, people are so spoiled because they have everything available to them. When God said "let there be light," it seems to have been directed to Americans. We have light, water, good roads, good hospitals, high-tech equipment, welfare, helicopters (to fly inmates to hospitals with), food, clean prisons, schools in prisons, programs, and even jobs for inmates.

Consider this scenario: In prison you are in charge of other inmates, who report to you; you direct and control them. You have power and move with authority and respect. When you are released from prison, things change. You face the reality of life. On the street, you are regarded as an exconvict. No one trusts you. Employers are hesitant to give you a job. You are shadowed by shame, humiliation, and lack of respect from people. After a while, you remember how inmates respected you in prison. At this point you might think, "You know what? I'm done with this. I just can't take it anymore." Then you end up back in prison.

If you cannot afford cable television in the outside world, you can come to prison and get it free of charge. If you cannot afford medical insurance, you can get medical for free as a prisoner. If you are too lazy to work, you just come to prison and eat free food. If you become very sick, especially with a heart condition, the criminal justice system will fly you to a big hospital. Now tell me: Wouldn't you rather choose prison in America? In other countries, when people go to prison, they lose weight. In America, when people go to prison, they gain weight. So does this mean that the country encourages bad behavior? I don't think so. It's just that the commodities we have are becoming disadvantageous to us and to the society as a whole.

77

Parents

Parents are the foundation of good behavior. When the father and the mother are both in prison, where will the children go? Children look up to their parents. They learn so quickly, and that's why it is so hard to avoid incarceration when their mentors are already taking that route.

Some parents don't tell their children that offenses like shoplifting are punishable by law. I applaud one woman, Linda, for what she did when she found out that her children had stolen something from a store. She and the children came home from a supermarket one Monday evening, and she saw her children all had Chap Stick, chewing gum, and nail polish that she did not remember buying. The children were between the ages of three and six years old. She asked the children, "Who bought those things for you guys?"

They answered, "We took them from the store."

Guess what this woman did? She told them to get ready, that she was taking them to the police. They thought she was playing. She put them in the car and started driving to the police station. This is when they knew it was actually serious. They started begging, "Mommy, please; Mommy, please." The car arrived at the police station. The children were crying, saying that they were really sorry and they didn't want to go to jail. They basically asked for a second chance. They got to the police before the plea for a second chance was granted.

After threatening them with the police, Linda took them back to the store to return those items. Guess what? A big lesson was learned. When parents don't condone theft or shoplifting, their children will know that it is bad to steal and if you do it, you will go to jail. So when children think it's okay to take anything you want from a store, you teach them that it's not okay.

Parents have the power to influence their children, but the influence can be positive or negative. When it's positive, everyone benefits; when it's negative, prison tends to be the end product. Think about this: When parents are on drugs, they do drugs in front of the children. After doing drugs, they fight and verbally abuse each other, still in front of the kids. After a while, government agencies, such as the Child Protective Services (CPS), intervene and take away the children. These children are taken to foster homes, where they are raised by different people altogether. Nothing is the same anymore. Treatment is not the same, and even the love of family might not be there. Some foster parents care about the money they get from the government and not the children under their care. Right before these children hit their eighteenth birthday, it's time to phase out of the foster care system. At this point, where do these children go? At eighteen and nineteen years of age, youth still need guidance; otherwise, it's a likely time to make a variety of bad decisions.

This elaboration on foster homes is because my light research provided a shocking result—that 70 percent of inmates have a connection to foster care. What point then am I making here? Many children raised in foster homes do not get the best home training, education, and moral principles. They have no one father or mother to listen to or to be afraid of, and when they phase out of the program, they tend to settle for prison life as their best alternative.

Their biological parents, who are supposed to be their first teachers, are already in prison. Possibly some of the foster parents are too.

Who do you hold accountable at this point? Do you hold the foster child, the biological parents, or the foster parents accountable? When the biological parents fail their children, they face the consequences, which are regrettable ones, because it's out of their own negligence or abuse that they lose their children to foster homes.

The liability is shared, however. Foster parents, who have been entrusted with a vital role and a high degree of responsibility, should never go unpunished when they have failed to provide for the basic needs and care for the children. If you mess up along the line as a foster parent, it's like a slap in the face to the government. You have been deemed capable and responsible for a soul, and you are not supposed to let the soul slip and perish. It is more devastating than rotting in prison.

Why should we take the leniency of the government for granted? Just because you get almost everything you need in prison doesn't mean your entire generation should accept life in prison as a norm. I understand you messed up, but guess what? You need to fix it. We, the prison officials, need to decongest the prisons by all means because it might reach a point when people will start getting really sick as a result of prison congestion. In conclusion, the system, society, and family all have roles to play in keeping our citizens out of prison.

According to statistics from the Bureau of Justice (Patrick A. Langan, PhD, David J. Levin, PhD):

- Among nearly 300,000 prisoners released in 15 states in 1994, 67.5% were rearrested within 3 years.
- During 2007, a total of 1,180,469 persons on parole were at risk of reincarceration.
- Released prisoners with the highest rearrest rates were robbers (70.2%), burglars (74.0%), larcenists (74.6%), motor vehicle thieves (78.8%), those in prison for possessing or selling stolen property (77.4%), and those in prison for possessing, using, or selling illegal weapons (70.2%).
- Within 3 years, 2.5% of released rapists were arrested for another rape, and 1.2% of those who had served time for homicide were arrested for homicide.
- The 272,111 offenders discharged in 1994 had accumulated 4.1 million arrest charges before their most recent imprisonment and another 744,000 charges within 3 years of release.

Points to Ponder

1. Prisons are overcrowded because many people have found home in prison as opposed to home in the outside world.

2. System, society, and family all play a role in the high recidivism of prisoners, but that is not an excuse for the prisoners. Avoid getting entangled with the system, by all means.

3. Victims want justice to prevail. The criminal justice system must implement the objectives of the police, the court, and the corrections team so as to measure up to the demands.

4. A victim is afraid of being victimized again and therefore wants the perpetrator locked up. Meanwhile the defense attorney wants the alleged perpetrator to be set free.

5. Foster care children are more vulnerable to crimes and prison than children raised by their biological parents.

6. Seventy percent of inmates have a connection to foster homes—either as a child or as a parent.

7. Parents should caution their children that shoplifting is an offense punishable by law instead of encouraging them to steal.

8. Whatever children learn while growing sticks.

9. Nurture a child to hate evil so we may once again enjoy a safe world, free of atrocities.

CHAPTER 9

JUST BE VIGILANT

Having seen the happenings of today's dangerous world, you don't need a soothsayer to tell you to watch out. Watch your surroundings wherever you are. You can do that by paying attention to suspicious behavior, movements, or changes in a person's attitude or character.

In the cause of vigilance, ask for a discerning spirit so you may know when to detach from unworthy relationships. Nobody is telling you to be an enemy to your friends, but it is important to know when to draw the line. It's better to be safe than sorry.

Jealousy over what others have is a big part of human life. Some people say it is normal for one to be jealous as long as the person refrains from taking it to the next level. I strongly disagree, and I will always argue that it is not normal nor natural. God never created us to kill our brothers or friends out of jealousy. There really shouldn't be any reason to be jealous of your friends only because they have something you don't have. You stand and complain; you compete and contest. You think they don't deserve what they have.

Perhaps when a friend was awake in the middle of the night studying, you snuggled under a comforter, enjoying your night's sleep.

Right after your friend graduated, you began your underground war. The supernatural eyes see what other eyes cannot see. Everything done in secret comes to light at the appointed time, and it comes with consequences.

Jealousy is a topic of concern because it has brought about widespread calamities in the world. This is another reason to stay as vigilant as possible in order to know when to draw the line on friendship. A discerning spirit can help you avoid going to that same place your friend used to take you to. When said friend calls you to meet up, your answer should be "Not anymore." Even in the military, when someone is jealous of you, he kills you on a battlefield and blames it on friendly fire. So there is a need to be vigilant and avoid supporting each other in jealous rants about other people.

Men kill their wives, and women kill their husbands. Parents kill their children, and children kill their parents. Siblings kill each other, and uncles encourage nephews to kill strangers. The DC sniper who turned out to be a minor killed pedestrians on his uncle's urging. The "Baseline" Serial Shooter killed motorists, gas station victims, and many unlucky people on the street. Even though he is locked up and on death row in the Arizona State Prison Complex in Florence, that does not change the fact that several human lives have been wasted for no reason.

The time for total dependence on the government for our safety and protection is gone. The incident of 9/11 should be an eye-opener for us. I strongly believe we have to help the government help us. You have every right to report any suspicious behavior or information about violent plans to government agencies, like the police departments, the Federal Bureau of Investigation (FBI), Central Intelligence Agency (CIA), and so forth.

I went to the mall one day with my wife; I suspected an awkward movement from one tall man, who kept pacing in the Dillard's cosmetics department. He was basically spraying all the tester colognes they had out on the counter. When I noticed something odd about him, I told my wife to stay clear just in case he opened fire. It's true what Shakespeare said in *Macbeth,* that "there is no art to find the mind's construction in the face," but it's better to be safe than sorry.

I am not saying you should judge or condemn everyone you see, but when you see a sign that speak evil about someone, just stay away from the person. The red flag is always vivid. You can't go wrong applying caution. Don't wait for it to happen. Clarke's commentary taken from 1 Peter 5:8 says, "Be vigilant—Awake, and keep awake; be always watchful; never be off your guard; your enemies are alert, they are never off theirs."

Luke 21:36 (NIV) says, "Be always on the watch, and pray that you may be able to escape all that is about to happen, and that you may be able to stand before the Son of Man." In a major disaster, there is always a victim. There is always a survivor too, but when was the last time you said, "This victim could have been me." Of course, it could be anyone, but for some reason we always escape—just watch and pray because "it is not of him that willeth, nor of him that runneth, but of God that showeth mercy" (Romans 9:16, KJV).

When you are boarding an aircraft or about to make any trip, listen to your instinct so you know when to say no. If you have to miss a flight and board another one, so be it. If you have to reschedule your trip either by land or sea, please do so. But in all things, we have to watch and pray so that when the enemy is in front, we shall be at the back. And when they are at the back, we shall be in front.

Be vigilant so you know when not to accept an evil gift. There are different kinds of gifts: good and evil ones. Seek discernment to know which is which. Don't take monetary gifts from a dangerous source because that money will yield dangerous fruits. Some incidents, like natural disasters, we cannot avoid, but how prepared are you to face those unavoidable situations when they happen? Some disasters are more precarious than others, but the magnitude of each determines the severity for victims. Earthquakes, hurricanes, tornadoes, and snowstorms are bound to happen, but my question is, "What should one do in such cases?"

- Prepare your mind for uncertainties and emergencies.
- Always pay attention to the news, especially weather forecasts.
- Keep a store of water at all times. Research has shown that humans can survive for only three days without water.
- Build your house, windows, and doors to meet the standard precautionary measures of the area you live in.
- Always maintain a working cell phone.
- Evacuate if need be. Some people stay to see what will happen despite evacuation orders.
- Most importantly, watch and pray.

"Touch not mine anointed and do my prophet no harm" (Psalm 105:15 KJV). Remember not to mess with God's servants because in them there is special power. If you mess with them, you are asking for danger, and when that danger comes, you will run to them to pray for you. Beware! Don't say that I didn't warn you, because some dangers we actually cause ourselves.

Returning to the discussion of prison, there is probably no more suitable place to use the phrase "just be vigilant." As Charles Ryan said, "Remain vigilant and focused on your duties, the behavior of the inmate population, and first and foremost, the safety of yourself and fellow staff." When you work in a prison, you have to watch your surroundings. You have a key set and a radio as well as other gadgets at all times. You must always make sure they are in your possession. Your radio is your lifeline. If anything happens to you or your fellow staff, you have to use your radio to save a life. In a situation where you have been rendered incapable of speaking, you have to push the man-down button. This button will automatically alert the main control officer that someone is in distress, without your speaking. Your location will be traced immediately for rescue.

Never let an inmate take your key set or radio away from you. The day you are overpowered by any of them and your gadgets are taken should be the end of your career—if you survive. If you are considering a career in law enforcement, you have to be the most careful person. Without vigilance and caution, I consider prison the most dangerous place to work. But with the application of caution and vigilance, carefully abiding by the rules and regulations, prison is safer than other public places.

When you are a newbie, inmates will tempt you to give them your keys so they can help you open the trap which you have been struggling to have open. But woe unto you if you succumb to such manipulation! Be vigilant and keep your things on you at all times.

Many correctional officers talk among themselves loudly, to the detriment of their privacy. When you make the decision to work at prison, you are choosing to talk less so that inmates will not penetrate your private life. It's risky to do so. Without any malice toward inmates, I seriously recommend drawing that line. Just don't play with fire because it's capable of burning you without looking back. Don't get too comfortable because you are there for a mission. You can't compromise your mission with friendship. There is definitely a time and place for everything.

Points to Ponder

1. In today's dangerous world, we are all expected to help the government in its effort to protect the nation.

2. You need to be vigilant at all times so you know when there is danger.

3. If you are prison staff, you don't need a soothsayer to tell you that without vigilance and carefulness prison is one of the most dangerous work environments.

4. Make necessary preparations for potential emergency situations.

5. Pay attention to the news and weather channels so you know when they say to evacuate.

6. When you are advised to evacuate, don't wait to see it first.

7. Jealousy is a sin and can lead to death.

8. Talk less because even the walls have ears.

CHAPTER 10

LIVING ABOVE MISERY

Based on my perspective, misery is a state of emotional distress, which can be caused by suffering, poverty, emotional trauma, bad marriage, or a poor attitude. Life is what it is, so hating yourself and hating everyone around you has never, and will never, solve problems. Many people find themselves in dejection and denial because of past experiences. Some of the things they complain about are supposed to have made them feel the way they feel, but the bottom line is that a pity party has never changed anything for anyone. It rather complicates matters.

When I read *Help Me I'm Married* by Joyce Meyer I found out that the author repeatedly narrated how her father sexually abused her. Thank goodness she has grown past the condition of dejection and has embraced God's love as she now enjoys her ministry as well as her loving and God-fearing husband, Dave. Of course, an experience like this is capable of causing emotional trauma, but, she didn't give up in living her life to the fullest. She chose to live above misery in order to enjoy what God has in store for her and her loving family.

Rita Ghatourey said, "Our background and circumstances may have influenced who we are, but we are responsible for whom we become." That's why I believe that some people actually have every reason to feel dejected, but I have also learnt that God's love supersedes every condition you have been subjected to.

You just have to let go and let God. Ask yourself, "How long am I going to live in this misery? How long am I going to remind myself of what he or she did to me in the past?" This is when animosity builds up. Animosity creates a bad attitude, and a bad attitude adversely affects every area of your life.

The most miserable individuals are those who are never happy when their friends are advancing in life. When you think that your friend is counting two while you are still counting one, wake up from your slumber and start counting two! It's not rocket science. If you cannot keep up with the pace, accept it graciously. Sitting back and murmuring about it does not make any positive difference in your life. It rather provokes anger and animosity. Be happy for others.

I have often noticed that singing or dancing takes away anxiety, tension, frustration, anger, misery, depression, and all other emotional and psychological imbalances in human life. Excessive drinking does not take care of these problems but can rather compound the issues by making you do things that you might regret when you become sober. Please try dancing or singing instead.

We have the power to take charge of our happiness. You just need to find what makes you happy and do it. It can be really stressful in this country, especially when all we do is work, work, and work. "The happiest of people don't necessarily have the best of everything; they just make the most of everything that comes along their way" (Karen S. Magee).

I pay a little extra on my satellite television bill because I have come to realize that watching soccer gives me happiness in today's busy lifestyle. I use my soccer channels to relax. I sometimes get upset that my wife doesn't like to sit and watch with me, but the truth is that what you like might not be what your spouse likes. You cannot change that; however, please don't let anyone deprive you of that one thing you like, as long as it's not a bad habit and it doesn't control you. My wife recently asked me, "Now that the EPL games are over, what are you going to do?" (The EPL is the English Premier League.) Guess what my answer was? "Well, as EPL finishes, the World Cup is around the corner." I anticipate watching soccer at its best in the world's most renowned soccer country, Brazil. I am indeed looking forward to seeing something great this summer. Then after the World Cup, there comes another EPL season. I think life is good; we just need to figure out the best approach for a happy life and forget about the dangers of this generation for a minute.

I have taken my wife to a live soccer game in Phoenix, to watch Christiano Ronaldo of Portugal (and Real Madrid FC) play against Los Angeles Galaxy. I have taken her to the same stadium to watch the Phoenix Suns play basketball against the San Antonio Spurs. We have watched many live sports, including boxing and bowling competitions. What I am emphasizing here is not how I have the best life but how sports in general, and especially soccer, have helped me cope with the pressures of life. Life can be overwhelming if all you do is work and sleep, work and sleep; you go to a social gathering or church and instead of getting rid of tension by dancing, you just sit and look at people. You go back home with a heavy heart because you made absolutely no effort to get rid of those troubles of the mind.

I have noticed that when people have financial predicaments (basically everyone at some point), their faces tend to show that they are going through something hard. You see it written on their faces as if someone died. They are probably better off than their next-door neighbor, but they won't notice because the next-door neighbor is always cheerful. Life is too short to not make the best of it.

5 Contributing Factors to Living in Misery

- ❖ Sickness
- ❖ Hardship
- ❖ Financial predicaments
- ❖ Marriage struggles
- ❖ Emotional trauma

5 Possible Solutions to Living in Misery

- ❖ God's love
- ❖ Dancing
- ❖ Singing & Laughing
- ❖ Get involved in what you like
- ❖ A positive attitude

Points to Ponder

1. Many factors and conditions can render someone miserable, but God's divine love is capable of healing your bad memories.

2. A bad attitude adversely affects every area of your life.

3. Choose not to live in misery because the world is already filled with dangerous activities and evil deeds. Your personal contribution to it will make it worse.

4. Make sure you are not part of the people who inflict pain on.

5. Even though some people have reasons to be miserable, others have chosen to live in misery just out of their own bitterness of heart.

6. Jealousy contributes to misery.

7. Discover what makes you happy and do it because life is too short to not make the best of it.

8. Singing or dancing takes away anxiety, tension, frustration, anger, misery, depression, and all other emotional and psychological imbalances in human life.

CHAPTER 11

SURVIVING THE DANGER

When trees hear about danger, they remain where they are, but when humans hear about danger, they make a move. As humans, we tend to run away from anything we perceive as danger because we don't want to be afflicted and because we know we are capable of avoiding some dangers, if not all.

Life itself is full of danger, and I have noticed that, out of paranoia, some people disengage from the happenings of today's world. In so doing, life becomes meaningless and boring. Hatred takes over the mind, and violence is the result. When you are isolated because of fear, your mind starts to think of evil. That is when it starts to plot evil against humanity.

On the other hand, affliction and catastrophe prove our ability to show resilience to adversities and danger. Dangerous situations tend to reshape our lives because it is then that we seek God. We want him to intervene; therefore, we start to draw closer to him. I have also noticed that when things are going just the way we expect, we have little or no desire for God. Therefore, in a way, I can say that danger is necessary because it gives us a good reason to know God and do his will.

As a matter of fact, if you pay attention to the news, there is no single day you will not hear about one bad incident or another. Accidents and violent incidents of all kinds happen, as do breakouts of disease. There is danger all over the world, and this signifies something to me. Ask yourself, "Why is it so rampant these days, or has the world been like this all these years?"

Nigeria was once listed as one of the happiest countries in the world. Today, we cannot say the same. That country where some of us grew up has turned into a den of lions, a center of terrorists. That was unheard of back in the day.

There was a bomb blast that killed seventy-one people instantly and injured dozens of others in Abuja, Nigeria. The bomb was said to be buried underground while another source said it was planted underneath a bus. Either way, it was planted by someone. Speculation has it that Boko Haram is responsible for the deadly act. Boko Haram is a terrorist group that recently emerged in northern Nigeria. This is to make sure there is no peace in the world. It ignites the issues of nepotism, tribalism, and war between religions. My cousin, Chioma, who lives and works in Abuja, survived the danger, which was said to be one of the deadliest terrorist attacks in Nigeria. I thank God for his protection of my cousin.

The same Boko Haram is also responsible for the abduction of 276 schoolgirls in their Chibok boarding house in Nigeria. The atrocity was done on the same day to mark the viciousness of the extremists.

Engineer Emeka Nwankwo took it upon himself to spearhead a peaceful rally with the cry "Bring Back Our Girls" in Phoenix to create awareness, pray, and show support for the girls. He printed red T-shirts that were worn by whites, blacks, and Hispanics as they conducted an extensive march at the Arizona State Capital. This rally was covered by many local television news channels. Those girls are not alone. With God and with the help of America, Britain, Israel, and other concerned countries, our girls will survive the danger.

I know someone who vows she will never use her credit cards online or at a gas station pump. She believes that it is just too dangerous because hackers highjack your information from the Internet, gas pump machines, and so on. But I ask, how long are you going to run?

By avoiding the use of online shopping and online bill pay, you are depriving yourself the joy and convenience of living in an advanced world. We have to live a normal life while we maintain conscientious awareness of our surroundings. Don't be afraid of danger, but be ready to survive the danger when it comes. Prepare your mind and believe in God's protection.

You survive danger by applying the best security measures at your workplace, regardless of where you work. In prison, as you work toward the goals and missions of the department or facility, you should selfishly focus on your personal protection. Always go around with your personal protective equipment (PPE).

As a hospital worker, in your effort to help patients recover, you should understand that your health is important as well. You have to be healthy in order to take care of sick people. Therefore, you need to pay special attention to the needles you use for injections and infusions. You need to avoid direct contact with bodily fluids. Most importantly, pray before you go to work.

Although there is danger everywhere you go, you should also bear in mind that "the chief danger in life is that you may take too many precautions," as Alfred Adler said. You survive danger by making sure that a working cellular phone is handy at all times.

If only we could all get along, the dangers of the world would be significantly minimized. Human beings cause more than half of the dangers we face. People devise evil and carry improvised weapons. When a country is fighting to take over another, innocent individuals are losing their lives in the process. Many people have chosen violence over peace, to the detriment of the poor masses. The rich stay protected in their mansions with security guards, while the poor suffer from hunger and lose their lives to bombs while in search of food. People devise harm against even friends and relatives.

I use the title "Surviving the Danger" for this last chapter because, after all is said and done, our goal is to survive in this dangerous world. I hope we now agree that, despite existing in a world that is sometimes too dangerous to imagine, we still have the tools to escape danger and maintain a normal lifestyle. But most importantly, some dangers are made to draw us closer to God. That is a point to always bear in mind.

You need not be a coward to survive, but you shouldn't be a dead hero either. Take precautionary measures.

Ways to Survive the Danger

- Stay out of trouble
- Pay restitution
- Seek reconciliation
- Eat well and exercise right
- Embrace God.

Stay Out of Trouble

Since most of my work experiences have revolved around the Department of Corrections, I turn to that in my writing. I asked one inmate, whose entire family is in prison, "Is it really too hard to stay out of trouble?" This is what he said:

> Mr. Okafor, are you kidding me? This is all I know, man. I was born and raised in trouble. I started going to Juvenile Corrections when I was nine years old. I started smoking and doing drugs, engaging in gang fights and having group sex at twelve years. All of a sudden you are telling me to stay out of trouble at twenty-nine years. It's too late, man. I had been released before and there was nothing to do. I mingled back with the same group of friends I had always known. No one else wanted to give me a chance, so I went right back to selling drugs, and here I am again in prison.

Now the inmate's father is dead (after some prison time) and the mother is alive but in anguish because all three of her sons are in prison.

Based on the things I have heard so far, many offenders blame their situation on their parents. Some parents just didn't lay a good foundation for their children. They introduced them to their unhealthy lifestyle. Therefore staying out of trouble starts with the parents. This inmate has seven children right now, but he has nothing to teach or offer them. It's a chain reaction whereby they end up like daddy because there is no one guide them.

Please consider this scenario. Let's say a person sexually molested a child or had sexual intercourse with a sixteen-year old minor ten years ago. A minor is anyone less than eighteen years of age. One day, the offender finds Jesus and becomes a born-again Christian. He prays for God to forgive his sins, but also prays that what he did ten years ago is not revealed.

This is what happens. If the victim decides to tell someone else what happened ten years ago and that person reports it to the police, believe it or not, the offender is going to prison for at least ten years for committing a dangerous crime against children. I have actually seen someone who decided to man up and turn himself in to the police for molesting his own child. He has now been sentenced to ten years and the military sentenced him to another ten years. So he will serve a total of twenty years. Please try your best to stay out of trouble. Don't even start because I have seen how hard it is to truly leave the prison cycle once you are in.

When you make up your mind to stay out of trouble, you automatically save yourself the trauma of spending ten years or more incarcerated. *Survive the danger by saying no to troubles.*

Pay Restitution

Restitution is necessary no matter your religious status or spiritual level. Let's say you stole some money, either by trickery or by force. When you later decide to repent, it's still your obligation to pay back what you stole from a person or group. That is the meaning of restitution.

We all want God to forgive us our sins, but we also forget that some sins have consequences, regardless of whether it is forgiven or not. In high school, there was a debate about whether pen-stealing is more devastating than highway robbery. Both sides generated some interesting points, but there was indeed a strong argument that supported the notion that the pen-stealing (which could be seen as a white-collar crime) is capable of causing death, poverty, or everlasting pain to the individuals involved. Think before you act.

All I can do is stress the need to avoid causing harm to ourselves. Human beings are looking for any excuse to inflict pain on others, but when your hands are clean, nothing will affect you.

For the inmates, we take restitution automatically from their income. They have no choice but to pay it. But out in the world, you are considered a free person and therefore are not mandated to pay back the person you took advantage of. This is only because you were not caught and convicted. But since you know your past, it's your obligation to fix what you have broken by arranging to pay back what you have taken consciously and unconsciously.

Reconciliation

There is nothing wrong with trying to reconcile with your brother or friend. Some people think it makes them weaker, but that's certainly not true. It actually makes you the stronger person. Making up with someone you offended or someone who offended you settles a lot of vengeful acts. If a person is planning evil against you for what he or she thinks you did wrong, reconciling might stop the evil plans. Makeups stop break-ups, and some break-ups result in dangerous attacks.

I have heard that the greatest political squabbles are solved by violence, but in my opinion, dialogue is the best approach to reconciling disputes, especially among brothers. If you are aware of any trespass you have committed against your brother, you have a responsibility to go to him and seek his forgiveness. Should you not attempt reconciliation, this will hinder your relationship with God. Your worship, your prayers and service, to the Lord will not be acceptable. "Therefore if you bring your gift to the altar, and there remember that your brother has something against you, leave your gift there before the altar, and go your way. First be reconciled to your brother, and then come and offer your gift" (Matt. 5:23–24).

Reconciliation creates an atmosphere of peace. It also creates the fellowship and camaraderie that you might need to keep moving during tough times.

Eat Well and Exercise Right

Of course everyone knows they *should* eat well and exercise right. It might sound simple, but it's not easy to do. It means maintaining a balanced diet and actually eating your meals at the right time. Many of us have formed the habit of eating too late. Many of us prefer heavy meals all at once and still maintain three square meals a day. It is equally bad. Many meals eaten sparingly is perfect.

The major problem we have is exercising. I have noticed that it is one of the most difficult things to do; however, it helps so much if you really want to stay out of danger. You cannot imagine how dangerous it is to be obese. It simply shortens your lifespan and complicates your health issues. Dieting and exercising are the two most essential safety precautions that we often take for granted because we are busy. I remember what my doctor (Dr. David Lawson) told me one day: "If you don't have time to exercise, when you get sick, you will have time." He said, "Even if it's thirty-minute walk a day, it goes a long way."

Embrace God

They say one person with God is a majority. Embracing God empowers you to experience God's love. And God's love supersedes all emotions. Running to him gives you guidance and protection, which ultimately help you overcome dangers. God himself is love, and with that love, who in the world can be against you to the extent of having power over you? Our jealous God will not sit back and watch you be swallowed by the dangers of the world.

When you pay attention to the news, it's so easy to say there is no God. When 276 Chibok schoolgirls got abducted in Nigeria, their parents surely asked many questions and the world said many prayers, but things like this should not make you doubt the existence of God; rather, it should make us seek his face more than ever because we are indeed witnessing some serious signs of dangerous situations.

I hereby conclude by emphasizing that the challenges of life should draw us closer to our creator rather than draw us away. Events and happenings all over the world tend to highlight the helplessness and the futility of our knowledge as mankind. This should prompt everyone to seek God. Embracing God, therefore, helps in surviving dangerous times.

Points to Ponder

1. Humans are capable of running away from danger because God created us with a higher degree of intelligence than other living organisms.
2. We have ability to survive some dangerous situations, but we have to pay attention to detail.
3. Don't be afraid of danger, but be ready to survive the danger when it comes.
4. At your place of work, always take the precautions recommended.
5. If you are medical staff, your health and safety come first.
6. If you are correctional staff, pay attention to your surroundings at all times.
7. We have to try hard to live a normal life while we maintain conscientious awareness of our surroundings.
8. Danger is good in a way because it draws us closer to God and reshapes our lives.
9. Out of paranoia some people have decided to disengage from the happenings of today's world.
10. Affliction and catastrophe prove our ability to show resilience to adversity or danger.

ABOUT THIS BOOK

Writing is a creative art. Grammatical fluency and vocabulary prowess are not sufficient to produce an interesting, easy-to-read, comprehensive piece of work called a "book" when the author lacks the organizational acumen to arrange and create something out of nothing.

I realized this important fact while putting together this little work. A person's natural talents and skills are there, and they may never go away, but they can be sharpened by effort. In other words, one can always do better. There is room for improvement in everything we do in life.

This book includes examples from personal life experience to educate readers on how to survive in today's dangerous world. There are also techniques on how to prepare for inevitable emergency situations. This book elucidates how dangerous the world is, but it also teaches how to live a quality life, regardless of the danger. It addresses the need to remain committed to work, participate in social activities, and continue to enjoy family and friends. There should be moderation in everything we do.

As you read *Surviving in a Dangerous World,* I hope you are able to make use of one or two things, especially from the true stories I used to put my points across. My goal is to keep reaching out to the world in my own little way; I hope someone will be blessed.

ACKNOWLEDGMENTS

I thank God for the opportunity to write my second book, *Surviving in a Dangerous World*. I truly appreciate my family and friends, who, out of kindness, support me in all areas. I will always say that it takes a community to accomplish a goal like this, and you are the community. Be blessed wherever you are.

I give credit to my wife, Linda, who took the photograph for the front cover of my first book. Many people have asked me, "Who is the professional photographer that did such an awesome job?" So I believe she deserves to be recognized.

Dr. and Mrs. Uche Okafor, I applaud you for your tremendous support for my first book. You made it a success. I thank you, and may God bless you. Dr. Michael Igwe, your ideas and recommendations to make this book the best it can be are highly appreciated. I could not ask for a more suitable individual for this kind of work. Be blessed.

Many people have contributed to my work without knowing it. Therefore, I appreciate those who contributed consciously and unconsciously. May God bless you all. I will once again recognize the person who laid the foundation of writing in me. My father, the late Chief J. U. Okafor is not here anymore to see that I continue to do what he taught me to do, but I know he's happy where he is.

ABOUT THE AUTHOR

Tochukwu Okafor received his master's degree in public administration with a specialization in law and public policy from Walden University in Minneapolis, Minnesota. He currently works for the State of Arizona, managing correctional programs for the Arizona Department of Corrections (ADC).

He is a member of the American Society for Public Administration (ASPA), American Correctional Association (ACA), and Arizona Probation, Parole and Corrections Association (APPCA). Tochukwu is the author of *The Joy of Success: What It Means to Transform Success into Excellence.* He is married and has three children.

REFERENCES

Statistic Brain. "9/11 Death Statistics" Retrieved December 16, 2013.
http://www.statisticbrain.com/911-death-statistics/

Shaw, George Bernard. BrainyQuote.com. Retrieved March 20, 2014.
http://www.brainyquote.com/quotes/quotes/g/georgebern
386923.html#XV0ASDCDQQ3gPvew.99

Bureau of Justice Statistics. Retrieved March 26, 2014.
http://www.bjs.gov/index.cfm?ty=tp&tid=17

Explainer. Retrieved March 27, 2014.
http://www.slate.com/articles/news_and_politics/explainer/
2013/06/murder_rate_in_prison_is_it_safer_to_be_jailed_
than_free.html

Osteen, Joel. Retrieved December 14, 2013.
http://www.brainyquote.com/quotes/quotes/j/joelosteen446953.
html

Brofenbrenner, Kate. 1997. "Worker Turnover and Part-Time Employment at UPS." Retrieved January 14, 2014. http://digitalcommons.ilr.cornell.edu/cgi/viewcontent. cgi?article=1003&context=reports

Frontline. Retrieved April 28, 2014. http://www.pbs.org/wgbh/pages/frontline/locked-up-in-america/

ADC Policy. Retrieved April 28, 2014. http://www.azcorrections.gov/Z_dept_orders_1.aspx

Meyer, Joyce. "Help Me I'm Married." Tulsa, Ok: Harrison House.

www.tochukwuokafor.com

Okafor's first book, *The Joy of Success* was written to inspire the world to challenge the impediments of life.

MESA, Ariz. (PRWEB) May 09, 2013

In *The Joy of Success: What It Means to Transform Success into Excellence* (published by iUniverse), author Tochukwu O. Okafor's new motivational book, readers are given the tools they need to become successful in life.

The Joy of Success is a step-by-step guide that explains the meaning of success, considers what one must do to achieve it and offers practical advice about what to avoid in the process. Woven throughout the guide are true stories of transformation that occurred in the author's life that help support the notion that success is obtainable if one works hard and keeps one's eye on excellence.

Readers are also given instructions that will help them properly understand the concept of success. This takes into account emotional stability, financial breakthrough, attainment of goals, happiness in marriage, job satisfaction, discovering of talents, prosperity and much more.

"Excellence cannot be achieved without success," says Okafor. "Therefore, your success is not complete until you reach the level of excellence desired. If you're ready to take charge of your success, this guide offers you the motivation you need to achieve the success you want."

The Joy of Success
By Tochukwu O. Okafor
Hardcover | 5.5 x 8.5 in | 122 pages | ISBN 9781475984002
Softcover | 5.5 x 8.5 in | 122 pages | ISBN 9781475983999
E-Book | 122 pages | ISBN 9781475984019
Available at Amazon and Barnes & Noble